The INFJ Revolution

Reclaim Your Power

Live Your Purpose

Heal the World

By Lauren Sapala

ISBN: 978-0-9988536-6-6

Cover artwork by John Price

Also by Lauren Sapala

Nonfiction

The INFJ Writer:
Cracking the Creative Genius of the World's Rarest Type

Firefly Magic:
Heart Powered Marketing for Highly Sensitive Writers

Fiction

Between the Shadow and Lo
(Book One of the West Coast Trilogy)

West Is San Francisco
(Book Two of the West Coast Trilogy)

Introduction

Three years ago I wrote a little book called *The INFJ Writer*. I say "little" because that's honestly how it felt to me at the time. I got the idea for it and wrote the whole thing in a matter of months and I never conceived of it going out into the world as anything other than a simple writing guide for INFJ and INFP personality types.

But a funny thing happened after I published that book. I started getting messages from INFJs all over the world about how profoundly it touched them, and just about every message contained a personal story of how that person had struggled through life in one way or another before finding out they were an INFJ. After the discovery of their personality type, everything changed.

What didn't change, though, were the ongoing challenges that came with being an INFJ. In all the stories that people shared with me, the obstacles remained the same. The loneliness, the overwhelming sensitivity, the feeling of being a freak or an alien in a world that seemed to fit everyone except the INFJ. What also remained true for every INFJ was the deep calling they felt to find their life purpose and be of service to the world, if only they could conquer what was blocking them from moving forward in their lives.

As I received story after story from all these INFJs, I felt my own deep calling begin to grow. I knew I had to write another book for INFJs, one that wasn't just about writing or creativity, but that explored the more hidden problems, the darker feelings and dysfunctional patterns from which we all seemed to suffer. I knew, too, that I needed this book to show INFJs that things could change for us, that the world was already changing due to our newfound awareness of who we are and what we might be capable of—even if that awareness and capability is only just now pushing out of the seed, breaking the soil, and tentatively reaching for the light.

This is a different kind of book for INFJs. You won't find much here on the basics of personality theory or any in-depth explanation of the INFJ's function stack. Not only does it seem that most INFJs who find my books already know all that stuff anyway, but it can easily be found online with a quick search. This isn't a book that regurgitates everything that can be found through Google. Instead, this is a book of my own personal observations and theories about what it means to be an INFJ, how we invalidate and sabotage ourselves, and how we can stop. This is a book that talks about things like shamanism, Native American spirituality, and New Age philosophy. It's a book that, at its core, is built to shift the reader energetically by introducing new thought patterns and ways of seeing ourselves.

It's not a book for everyone.

But if you're an INFJ who wants to move up to the next level in your life, then it might be for you.

And if you're still with me, then let's begin.

PART I

BIRTH OF A REVOLUTION:

Getting Over Giving Our INFJ Power Away

CHAPTER 1

INFJs and Power: Why We Give It Away

For most of my working life, I have worked in offices. And in almost every office, I had the lowest position on the totem pole: I was the office admin. Sometimes my title was "office manager" and sometimes it was "executive assistant," which sounds better but really isn't because in a small office it's basically the same thing. I always fell into this sort of job because it was easy for me. I had all the traits to be good at it, naturally. I was organized and efficient, as well as discreet and personable. And I had another trait, or maybe "habit" is a better word for it, that particularly suited being in a low-paid, underappreciated office position: I routinely gave my power away to other people.

In 2016 though, I started noticing something about my life. It felt poor. Not that I was poverty-stricken, but I *was* broke. And being broke seemed to be a constant condition for me. I was always having trouble meeting my financial obligations and always juggling credit card debt. I was always cutting off this or that relationship with someone because I felt they were taking advantage of me, or I had suddenly discovered they were an energy vampire who was sucking me dry. I was always struggling to say no to people, and all too often saying yes when I really didn't want to.

I started doing a lot of inner work around money, and abundance. What surprised me was that along with that work came an interest in power. For the first time in my life, it was a concept I was consciously thinking about, and something I knew I needed to delve into deeper. Power, to me, meant an oppressive force. Power was something I saw as smothering, controlling, manipulative, and sometimes, abusive. I got uncomfortable around power. I didn't even like talking about it. I didn't want anything to do with it. When it came near me, I wanted to get as far away as possible.

Because I was so uncomfortable with power, my own or anyone else's, whenever it showed up I quickly handed it off to someone else. And I was always reluctant to take it back.

As I dug further into my problems with power, I started digging up the past. I had hardly spoken in my first years of elementary school, and I had always been labeled as shy. When I did start talking more, the things I said were often weird, precocious, or made other people uncomfortable. I asked hard questions and waited patiently for honest answers. Sometimes people awkwardly changed the subject and sometimes they just outright told me I was weird and made fun of me.

I found out early on, as every INFJ and INFP does, that the things I liked—the things that I loved and lit me up inside—were not interesting to other people. In fact, a lot of the time other people found those things horrifying, gross, uncomfortable, or just deadly boring.

Also, I was an empath. So, when someone had that horrifying, gross, uncomfortable, or bored reaction, I *felt* it. I felt a tightening in my own chest when my questions made them anxious. I felt the urge to cry in my own body when I unwittingly triggered a hidden emotional reservoir in another. And when people got angry, even if it wasn't my fault and didn't involve me in any way whatsoever, I felt every jolt and surge of that adrenaline cocktail run through my own veins.

This made me avoid anything that involved negotiation, and there was nothing I hated more than flat-out confrontation.

Giving my power away from the start seemed to be my safest option. If I gave my power away right out of the gate no one would need to negotiate with me, or get into confrontations, or have any big, hot, messy emotions around me that would zap my system, make me ill, and then leave me reeling for the next few hours or days. As a young INFJ, constantly giving my power away was the best option I could give myself at the time.

But then, I grew up. And this strategy not only stopped working, it started poisoning my life and undermining me at every turn. Staying invisible meant that my natural creativity felt stifled and smothered. Avoiding confrontation meant that I frequently got walked on and used. Giving my power away on a constant basis meant that my batteries were always running low, and I had to constantly dig myself deeper in debt—both financially and energetically—just to break even.

After I saw this, I started to see other little things, too. Little things that added up to big things. Like how sometimes I let other people answer for me, even when I had an opinion or preference that I wanted to express that differed from theirs. And how sometimes I said, "I don't care," or, "it's up to you," when I cared very much, in fact, and would rather it not be up to the other person. I thought about how I walked into rooms and walked down the street, how I tried to make myself as small and invisible as possible so that other people wouldn't notice me. I realized, too, how I had so strongly attached myself to certain identities—I was an introvert, an INFJ, a weirdo, and an artist—always making myself into someone who was on the fringe, misunderstood, unheard, and suffering.

As I was doing all this inner work around power, I began to focus my attention on another area that had been drawing me in for a while: shamanic studies. Since I was very young, I had instinctively felt that the Universe was made up of energy, much of it conscious, and as I'd gotten older and more in touch with myself, I'd found that I could feel different types of energy more strongly than I ever could before. As I started looking at the concept of power from a shamanic point of view, I began to see that maybe it wasn't an oppressive force, but instead, an energy that could be used as an oppressive force *if one so chose*. Possibly, power was *just* a force, like electricity, or any other form of energy, and whoever was using it at the moment could decide the best way for it to be harnessed and directed.

When I started thinking about power as electricity instead of oppression, my view entirely shifted.

Along with the shift, I gained clarity around my own issues with power and what I had been doing with it subconsciously. It was like I'd been put in charge of a gigantic battery that held enough juice to run an electric switchboard for a whole city, my city. Only, I doubted my own abilities so much that I refused to run the switchboard myself. Instead, I gave the job away to anyone who happened to wander by and wanted to play around with a switchboard. So, sometimes my city had all the lights on in the middle of the day when lights weren't needed, and sometimes the lights wouldn't work at night when they were needed the most. And sometimes, all the fuses blew, because I had let a totally crazy person be in charge of the switchboard and they went totally bonkers.

Up until this point in my life, I'd had no idea that power could operate in any other way.

Everything changed after I started experimenting with power using the shamanic point of view. I realized that no one ever needed to *get the power* in interactions with others, which is what I'd always thought before. Instead of *getting* the power, I only needed to *hold* the power. And I only needed to hold my own power. There was no need to try to steal another person's power in order to be empowered during any interaction, which is what I had assumed based on most of the power dynamics I had experienced in my life. The methods of trying to get the power and stealing someone else's power, in fact, are just two different ways to deal with power. They are both manifestations of the abusive, oppressive power strategies that I had witnessed so often in our culture and wanted no part of for myself.

I believe that almost every INFJ and INFP goes through similar experiences with power. We learn when we're very young that something about us doesn't "fit" with the rest of the population, and we pay the price for being our natural selves in the form of being mocked, ignored, or dismissed. We also get a tidal wave of emotional input from others and we don't know how to turn it off. So, we adopt the strategy of avoidance and, sometimes, total withdrawal and shutdown. We turn over our switchboard to other people, whoever wanders by and seems authoritarian enough. We give other people—much of the time narcissistic abusers—reign over our battery, and we leave it up to them on whether or not the lights come on at midnight, or at two in the afternoon.

However, the reality is that INFJs and INFPs come endowed with a unique set of traits that equip us to handle power beautifully, if we're brave enough to embrace it. We are people who consider situations from every angle and never rush to conclusions. Compassion and empathy sit high on our list of values and we will go to great lengths to ensure both are in place in all our relationships and interactions. We have a keen sense of justice and fair play, and consideration for those who *are* actually oppressed and powerless comes naturally to us. As long as we strive to be emotionally honest with ourselves and others, we don't need to be afraid that we'll end up abusing any amount of power that lands in our hands.

As with most things, the biggest obstacle holding us back from a healthy relationship with power is ourselves. In the next few chapters we'll explore all the different trademark ways INFJs and INFPs tend to give our power away to others. Once we examine and become thoroughly aware of our limiting beliefs around power, we can begin to break away from our culture's dysfunctional relationship with power. Then we can build a new power structure, on our own terms. The goal is to end up where we always needed to be: in charge of ourselves and ready to wield our power with both light and grace so that we can fulfill our highest potential as INFJs and INFPs, changing the world for the better.

CHAPTER 2

INFJ Anxiety: Why Most of Us Are Control Freaks

It was a beautiful Friday afternoon in San Francisco and I was sitting in the front window of a restaurant in one of the city's busier neighborhoods, waiting for my pick-up order to be ready. Every week I organized the company lunch for my office, which meant that I ordered all the food, set up our conference room for the meal, and was responsible for cleanup afterward. It was, in fact, one of the main reasons I had been hired. Among my many assistant duties, managing company lunch was one of the most important.

At this point, I had worked at the company for almost five years and had put together roughly 250 company lunches. We always had approximately 12 to 15 people on staff and company lunch was extremely casual. There was no definite time lunch needed to be served and no rigid expectations about how it should be done. Plus, I picked the restaurant each week, so I made sure to order from places that I knew would be easy to work with.

So, I'd had years of practice, done this thing hundreds of times, there was zero pressure to "get it right," *and* I had full control over all the details. Anyone would assume that I'd be sitting there with nothing more on my mind besides relishing the warm sunshine spilling in through the windows.

Instead, I was feeling anxious. And the anxiety was building. Right now, I was at a three or four on my own little personal anxiety scale, but my breathing was becoming shallower by the second, my shoulders were hiking up toward my ears, and my stomach was dropping. I anticipated that I'd be at a five or six soon. I probably wouldn't go *past* six, which was cool, but sitting steady at a six on my own little personal anxiety scale was no picnic either.

Why was I so stressed out?

Well, for one thing, I felt like I was late. There was no *definite* deadline of when lunch had to be served, but I *felt* like people started getting restless and hungry around 12:30 and it was already 12:35 and I was still at the restaurant. I still had to drive back to the office and set out all the food. Also, I had picked a new restaurant that day, an Indian place that got awesome reviews and so far had been wonderful, but that was, still, to me, *new*. And anything new tended to trigger my anxiety. On top of that, traffic had been intense on the way over and I'd had to parallel park on a busy street, necessitating that the cars behind me wait as I pulled into a tight squeeze of a parking space, and I could feel all the other drivers watching me as I parked.

So, I was late but not really, I was in a new restaurant, and I'd had to deal with traffic and parking in a big city. No big deal, right?

Well, that's the thing. I *knew* this would be no big deal for most of the population. And I also knew that when I got back to the office someone was bound to notice that I was stressed out and ask me about it and I would do that thing where I fake-smiled and shrugged and brushed the whole thing off. Because how could I explain that the combination of almost-late/new/intense-and-busy had quickly pushed me up to a five (*really* a six) on my own little personal anxiety scale? How could I even tell them that I *had* a personal anxiety scale that I used several times a day, and no, I did not learn this tool in therapy, it was something I grasped onto inside my own mind all by myself as a result of YEARS of dealing with massive anxiety, knowing that if I didn't have something to categorize and compartmentalize that anxiety I would probably go insane?

You just can't tell your (pretty much normal) coworkers all that.

However, in the years since that day at the restaurant I discovered something that has brought me overwhelming relief about my anxious self and what could possibly be wrong with me. It was the realization that every INFJ and INFP I've ever met suffers from anxiety. Sometimes it's severe and sometimes it's mild (and we're lucky if it's mild), but it's pretty much always there and it never really goes away. Some of us go to therapy and some of us take medication and some of us practice meditation, but it never really goes away. Some of us talk about it and blog about it and some of us keep it to ourselves and try to just get on with it but *it never really goes away.*

There are lots of theories out there on INFJ/INFP anxiety. We are Highly Sensitive People, obviously, so we pick up on more stimulation from our environment, and therefore, we become overwhelmed more easily. There is also the fact that introverts' brains are wired differently, so dopamine hits us harder and can also get overwhelming quickly and feel unpleasant. I get all that and I agree with all that. But I think there is more to it.

For INFJs and INFPs, there is another issue at play: boundaries.

When most people talk about boundaries they are referring to boundaries that exist in this concrete reality. Everyone has boundaries around their body, for instance, that are reflected by their own bubble of physical space. We might even go further sometimes and talk about emotional boundaries, which are technically outside of the physical, but still in the same territory. These are boundaries that most people can name, envision easily, and recognize when they are being violated.

But INFJs and INFPs are not most people. In addition to being Highly Sensitive People and introverts, we are also empaths. That means we are more sensitive than others to another type of boundary being crossed—the energetic boundary.

Empaths and non-empaths have vastly different experiences with human interaction. Someone who is not an empath might experience a negative, toxic person as unpleasant, or even a "real downer." They might come away from such a person feeling grumpy themselves or annoyed at dealing with them. But for an INFJ/INFP empath the game is changed. When toxic people come into our space we receive their negativity as an energetic poison and this poison lodges in our energy field like a lump of undigested food sits like a rock in someone's gut.

This kind of energy also doesn't have to come from someone who is obviously negative or toxic. We can pick up energy from anyone who is giving off a strong emotional signal *for any reason in any given moment.*

For many INFJs and INFPs the empathic process is wholly unconscious. It begins happening when we are very small children and continues on our entire lives. In fact, I wouldn't doubt that it begins from the time we're babies and we just don't have any memory of it. INFJs and INFPs are *receivers*, and we can receive any of the various emotional signals floating by. It's important to know, too, that the transmitters—the people giving off these signals—are also unconscious. They're mostly just regular folks who are going about their normal lives, reacting to things and having emotions. Not all of them are toxic people who need to be warded off or defended against with bubbles of white light (which has honestly never worked for me anyway).

Yes, there are psychic vampires out there and if you look around online you'll find all sorts of methods and strategies for dealing with them, but *most* people are not psychic vampires. However, that doesn't change the day-to-day reality of INFJ and INFP empaths. No matter what, we will always receive downloads of emotional data from others, whether we want it or not. Because, unless we're home alone, or with a trusted partner or close friends who act as a safe refuge for us, chances are we're somewhere like an office or a classroom or some other public space. Like it or not, in these types of situations our energetic boundaries are fucked with constantly by the emotional energy of the people surrounding us.

And *this* is the reason why INFJs and INFPs can get so controlling about things.

It doesn't seem to fit on the surface. At first glance, we can come across as quiet and low maintenance and very, very accommodating to others. But I guarantee that if you really get to know any INFJ or INFP you will quickly discover that we have a whole list of personal "rules" in place for how we like things done. We need our living space to be a certain way. We need our routines to be a certain way. And we always, always need our values honored and respected, in a certain way. If any of these things are disrupted then the anxiety kicks in. It starts as a one or a two on the scale but can increase rapidly, until sometimes it reaches that unbearable pitch where we're so anxious we feel like we're actually having an out-of-body experience.

This is the root of that anxiety. On a very deep, intensely intimate level, we feel that our energetic boundaries are tested, messed with, and violated on an almost constant basis. We feel that we don't have control over those energetic boundaries and we never have. Added to that, we feel like *we* are the weird person in the room for even having this problem in the first place. Other "normal" people don't seem to experience it and there is no language available to even talk about it. There is no way to discuss it, or explain the problem to others who are not like us. So, from an early age we learn to manage it by doubling down on our control mechanisms. We control our environment, our schedule, our routines, and we try to control our thoughts and emotions just as oppressively at times. Because controlling all these little things gives us at least a fleeting sense of empowerment. Proof that we aren't totally helpless against the onslaught of energy we feel every day from so many, many others.

It's no coincidence that trauma survivors also usually get obsessive about control. They've been violated too. Somewhere in the past, their boundaries were disrespected and abused, and so now, in the present, they devote a whole lot of energy to making sure the fences are built high and strong and monitored relentlessly, no matter the cost.

It's the same for INFJs and INFPs. Having our energetic boundaries crossed in so many ways, large and small, for our entire lives, *has* taken a toll. It *is* trauma from which we are still recovering.

And it is real.

I say that last part because so many INFJs and INFPs either blame themselves for being "too sensitive" or dismiss it all as something they're making up inside their own head. Once you start talking about any kind of psychic energy in our culture—emotional energetic transmissions from one soul to another or thought energy telepathically shared between brains—you get into dangerous territory where you might get the eye roll, or be scoffed at, or made to feel stupid or flaky or "less than" because you see the world in a different way that goes against the mainstream.

But it's time for INFJs and INFPs to come together and talk about these shared experiences. It's time for us to drop the shame that currently veils the honest truth we experience every day of our lives. Because it's very likely that we're going to give birth to intuitive children who will struggle with the same problems. It's guaranteed that there are young INFJ and INFP people out there *right now* who are going through experiences similar to what we went through in our childhood, adolescence, and young adulthood. The pain, the shame, and the inability to find a way out of it.

That day all those years ago when I was sitting in the sunlight at that restaurant, trying to look like I was just casually waiting for my order to be ready but really kind of dying inside as I fought off the anxiety I knew so well, I had no idea that I had such an obsessive need for control because I was an INFJ and an empath. I just thought something was wrong with me. If I had known then that I could learn how to manage my energetic boundaries more effectively, and that I didn't need lists of rules and rigid expectations to feel safe, I would have been able to enjoy the beautiful afternoon. Instead, I sat there and fretted and worried and beat myself up for being weird and anxious.

Once we understand that nothing is wrong with us and that it IS possible to let go of control and still protect ourselves energetically, everything changes. We go from being highly *anxious* INFJs and INFPs to highly *thriving* INFJs and INFPs. And the work we have to do to get there is well worth it.

CHAPTER 3

INFJs as Empaths: Why Boundaries Are So Hard for Us

As an INFJ or an INFP, maybe you figured out early on that you tend to soak up other people's emotions like a sponge. Maybe you realized all on your own that having firm energetic boundaries in place is an important factor in your self-care regimen. For me personally, I had no clue what was going on with my emotional system for many years. The only thing I knew was that *something* happened to me whenever I was around anyone experiencing strong emotions. My heart raced, I got shaky and sweaty, and sometimes dizzy. I also fainted a few times when I was young and became overwhelmed suddenly by someone else who was in pain.

I had always felt helpless to some degree around other people. I couldn't control their emotions and I couldn't control my own. I couldn't control what got dumped on me or when or how toxic it would be to my system. On top of this, I felt like I was probably crazy or emotionally unstable or something. My emotional life was just *so intense.* I had actual physical reactions to extreme emotional energy too, like getting the chills complete with chattering teeth in the middle of a hot summer day, or blinding headaches that came on out of nowhere.

When you add in my experiences with visions and hearing voices, it's clear why I was terrified that I might be mentally unstable. For many years, I lived with the feeling that I was walking on some sort of mental tightrope, and one day I would come tumbling down.

It wasn't until I started reading personal growth books and researching different personality theories and what it meant to be an introvert, and then strayed even further into the land of New Age philosophy, spirituality, and shamanism, that I really began to put all the pieces together for myself.

This didn't change the fact, though, that I was left with very little idea of what to do about it.

A lot of the stuff I found online about empaths told me to use the white light method, which I've already mentioned. Basically, the idea is to imagine a bubble of white light around yourself, a shield of sorts, that protects you from negative and/or intense emotional energy. Well, I tried it. A bunch of times. And it just never worked. I wasn't sure if I was doing it wrong or if I was just too skeptical about it in the first place, but I never got results with that method.

Then I fell back on my tried-and-true method for getting through rough spots in life: avoidance. After I found out I was officially an introvert, I read dozens of articles about how it was okay to retreat from the world to protect myself and recharge. I took this advice to the extreme and spent a few months doing very little other than going to work and then going straight home. This felt easy to me. I didn't mind turning down invitations to hang out with friends and avoiding all public activities. But, after a while, my relationships started to suffer. My friends let me know they were sad that they never saw me anymore, and even my husband, an INTJ, was complaining that he was getting bored sitting at home all the time.

So, I couldn't adopt the magical strategy of going out into the world as a fearless warrior surrounded by white light that made everything bounce off me, and I also couldn't use the more practical method of staying home all the time and thereby avoiding the whole mess of other humans and what they brought with them.

There had to be some middle ground in there somewhere.

And, after a bit more searching, I found it.

The first step was learning that I was an INFJ and then meeting and talking with other INFJs. They had all experienced the same things I had experienced, so I wasn't an isolated case. And it seemed weird that

I might be suffering from some sort of mental disorder and then all these other people who were the same personality type as me also happened to be suffering from the same mental disorder, so I felt I could safely rule out mental illness.

And really, I had always known, deep down, that I wasn't mentally ill. I might not have had the language or the skills to properly identify or talk about what was happening to me, but on a gut level, I knew that it was real and I was mentally healthy. I also knew, on that same gut level, that perhaps I was so conflicted over my experiences because I was surrounded by a larger culture that refused to recognize those experiences as valid and real.

So, just knowing—*really* knowing—that I wasn't mentally ill and that my experiences were similar to the experiences of other people of my same personality type, was incredibly comforting and liberating. This is one of the reasons I urge any INFJ or INFP to find an online community that works for them, whether it's an INFJ/INFP community, or one built for Highly Sensitive People or empaths. Knowing that you are not alone and hearing accounts from others of experiences that you thought were only happening to you, is a huge relief that I can barely even describe.

The second step is learning how to work with energy.

I've found that every person seems to take their own unique path when it comes to this sort of journey. My path led me to a man who was working as a clerk at a bookstore I frequented. I became good friends with him and then he became my mentor. He was almost 20 years older than me and had gone much further down the rabbit hole of exploring the energetic realm than I had. He taught me how to shift from trying to *think* my way through every challenge in life to *feeling and intuiting* my way through instead. Once I learned how to detach from my brain and stopped forcing myself to always use logic as my first choice in any situation, my world radically opened up in a new way.

Before, I had been viewing the "problem" as other people. My goal had been to ward off other humans and their messy emotions because those messy emotions felt too overwhelming to my system. All that changed when I learned how to work with energy, because suddenly I saw that there was no problem and so I didn't need to keep pouring myself into finding and executing a solution.

Instead of trying to "do something" when I was around other people who were having strong emotions—something like fix them, help them, shift them, counsel them, agree with them, disagree with them, protect myself from them, push them away, avoid them, or build a wall against them—I realized I could just do…*nothing.* I could be present, witness their emotional reactions, observe myself having the experience, and let it pass.

Then, after the storm had blown over, I could take some private time and space for myself, sift through the emotions that were floating around in my energy field, separate out what was mine and what was theirs, and then sit with it until that passed too.

This meant that all my old escape routes were closed to me. I couldn't pretend the bubble of white light was working for me (when it wasn't) and go into denial and suppression mode. And I couldn't block out everything (including my loved ones) by staying at home all the time and go into avoidance mode. Instead, I was choosing to continue having relationships with other people and then *working with the energy* of those relationships within myself.

This also meant that my traditional methods of INFJ control were disrupted. Sometimes things went off course and off schedule, and sometimes I landed in new environments with new people where I didn't know what to expect. But I found that as my energy skills got stronger, as I became more confident in my ability to observe energy—to identify what belonged to me and what belonged to someone else—and then to work with that energy in a way that ensured it kept moving and didn't lodge within me and get stuck there, *that* was when everything changed.

Then I started looking into other subjects, like shamanism and somatic therapy, and prayer and channeling. Venturing into these areas felt like I was leaving the safety of mainstream society behind and pushing into places that only the eccentric and weird (and possibly very wise) went. But it also felt like I was coming home. I had started out feeling and intuiting my way through life, but then had decided that was the wrong way to do things and so tried to force myself to swerve over to rationality and logic whenever possible. Letting myself *fully* feel and intuit, fully surrender to my own natural abilities, felt like such utter relief. I finally felt...free.

That's when I noticed my anxiety levels really started to drop, and so did my need for control. Suddenly, I didn't feel like I had to protect myself from other people. I felt like I was walking around whole and healthy, my core strong and centered, and my vision clear and focused. If someone got super angry around me, it still felt uncomfortable, but I could handle it. If someone came into my space and I saw they were a toxic person, it became much easier to move around them and not get so entangled. I had a language and a tool set to deal with the way I experienced the world and I wasn't afraid to use it. I wasn't constantly questioning if my experiences were real, or trying to brush them off and subtly invalidate myself in the process.

Suddenly, I had power.

Now, I believed in myself and I respected my unique experience of life. I was an emotionally-centered empath with amazingly accurate intuition. I could trust that. And I could trust myself.

Your journey may look different from mine, but no matter what form it takes, it's important that you follow your gut and what *feels* right to you. As an INFJ or an INFP, you've most likely already experienced a lot of disbelief or invalidation of your experiences by your friends or members of your family or collective society as a whole. Just because they can't understand your experience doesn't mean it's not real. Just because science doesn't yet have all the details worked out on how intuitive people operate doesn't mean it's not actually happening.

The most important takeaway from all this is maybe the most obvious one, and also the hardest to put into action. Let yourself *be* yourself. Listen to your intuition. Feel your way through situations. Move at your own (sometimes slow) pace and recognize what's emotionally yours and what belongs to someone else.

This is the beginning of the magic of energetic boundaries, and the beginning of the end of the tyranny of anxiety.

CHAPTER 4
INFJs as People Pleasers: Always Saying Yes When We Really Mean No

When I was in my mid 20s I worked at a private detective agency in San Francisco. It was my first office job and I was grateful to get it. I had no experience and was only hired because one of my old college friends already worked there and recommended me. I started out as the receptionist but then my old college friend left the company and I moved into her position, which meant I managed the surveillance team and also acted as righthand man to the boss.

My boss had a volatile personality, to put it lightly. He was an absolute tornado of a man—emotional, shrewd, unpredictable, and larger than life. He was one hundred percent an extrovert and loved nothing more than going out to business lunches and talking to clients on the phone all day. He also had a hot temper and a habit of smashing his desk phone into bits whenever he went into a rage.

I was fascinated by my boss. I genuinely loved him and was also intrigued by him. But his personality felt like a bulldozer to me. He rarely ever stopped moving long enough to participate in a real conversation. From day one, I had tried to stay invisible by melting into the background. This was something I had done all my life, but because my boss had such an aggressive nature and violent temper, I went even further with it than normal. After working there for only a short while, I ended up spending every minute in full-on people-pleasing mode.

People-pleasing: The toxic poison that seeps into a person's life and slowly consumes the vital organs until the person in question dies slowly and painfully from repressed rage.

Is this an over-exaggeration? Well, yes and no. I worked at the private detective agency for over two years, and when the boss and his wife took me out for lunch one day to thank me for all my hard work I felt dizzy and sick the entire time because waves of intense anger kept washing over me as we sat at the table. I had said "yes" so many times when I really should have said "no" that I had finally reached a point where I probably could have cold-bloodedly killed them both and never looked back.

Emotionally, it wasn't a pleasant place to be.

What made things worse, in my mind, was that I was well aware of the problem. I had struggled with people-pleasing my entire life. But although I knew this issue had a hugely detrimental effect on me, I also felt powerless to stop myself from doing it.

There are a variety of reasons that INFJs and INFPs fall prey to people-pleasing tendencies, many of them obvious. Both types are feelers, and so emotionally connecting to others is important to us. For INFJs, extraverted feeling is our auxiliary function. It's the "assistant manager" of the store, and just like most assistant managers, sometimes it does more work than the official boss. INFJs are extremely adept at observing how others react to us and then adjusting our own facial expressions, tone of voice, and body language to put them at ease, open them up, and invite trust and understanding.

But sometimes people-pleasing occurs as an accidental side effect of the INFJ's dominant function, introverted intuition, and the INFP's dominant function, introverted feeling. Because both introverted intuition and introverted feeling need a bit of time to gather data and process information, when an extrovert comes barreling into our space, talking a mile-a-minute and hurling all sorts of stimuli at us, we can become easily overwhelmed and say "yes" on autopilot before we even have a chance to think.

However, I believe the poison of people-pleasing for most INFJs and INFPs can also go deeper than either of these reasons.

In our culture today, emotional dysfunction is treated as something that is wrong and that can be fixed. It's something you get into therapy to "work on," and something you "move past." Sometimes it's something you take medication to treat. But, pretty much always, it's seen as something that is wrong and needs to be fixed, which implies that it's also something out of the ordinary. However, emotional dysfunction is as old as the age of humanity. I'm willing to bet that even the most primitive humans fought with their parents, suffered from sibling rivalry, and used all sorts of problematic emotional defense mechanisms to get through life.

Basically, everyone who has ever participated in a human relationship has dealt with emotional dysfunction in one form or another.

As intuitive, introverted feelers, INFJs and INFPs are deeply affected by the emotional lives of the people surrounding us. As empaths, we learn early on that other people's emotions can very quickly turn into landmines and catch us when we're least expecting it. Added to this is our natural facility for listening and a strong inborn tendency to show compassion to others. So, that means that not only are we the ones in the household who are usually the most affected by whatever level of screwed up our family is, but we're also the ones that everyone comes to when they need an empathetic ear, or even just an emotional dumping ground.

Some of us grow up with parents on the extremely negative end of the spectrum of emotional dysfunction: addicts and alcoholics, narcissists, abusers, and the like. And some of us just end up as the constant mediator between two family members who will never get along. But no matter where we, or our family, land on the dysfunction scale, we are almost always the ones who act as the "fixer," or the one who never makes trouble by going along with whatever is asked of us, at any time.

Once I realized this was true in my case (I had always been the mediator in my family), in true INFJ fashion, I went after a solution to the problem like a dog digging up a bone. But most of the information

I found on this topic proved disappointing. I started out hopeful, but with every new article I read I felt that old familiar feeling of "there's something wrong with me" coming back. Because almost every article either told me I needed to have better boundaries in place, or that I was codependent and needed to work on that, or both.

I tried to follow this sort of advice for many years, including during my time at the private detective agency. Whenever I found myself in people-pleasing overdrive, I analyzed exactly what had happened. I logically took note of where I went wrong, of how I had relapsed in my addiction to codependency. I vowed to do better next time, resolving to stop myself from saying "yes" to people when I really meant "no." But then it would happen all over again and I would be right back at square one, reading these articles about people-pleasing that told me all the same old things and really weren't making me feel better about any of it.

It took a very long time for me to understand that I wasn't an idiot when it came to getting this problem solved, it's that I was looking at it the wrong way.

Every time I fell into people-pleasing, I tried to solve the problem mentally. And every article I read online reinforced that approach. I was trying to use the tools of logic and reason to solve an *emotional* problem, and that's why those tools weren't working. Rational thinking is pretty much the religion of today's age, so it's no surprise that almost everything I found online urged me even further in this direction. Every time I felt stuck, my sources pushed me to "think harder" and "do better."

But I didn't need to think harder or do better. I needed to drop the mental approach and move into new territory with new tools that worked the best for me: my intuition and emotion. I needed to work with the energy of my whole being—mind, body, *and* soul. Not just my brain.

Using this new approach, I quickly found my body was one of my strongest allies. My brain frequently overrode the subtle signals I got from my environment, convincing me that I had no reason *not* to trust this new person I had just met, or that I should just forge ahead in a situation, even if my body was screaming at me that it was uncomfortable and needed to get out. But when I stopped relying so much on my mental tools and started listening to my body and treating it as a vessel that could communicate the deeper needs of my soul, I started getting loads of information about how to work with boundaries.

I realized that my body frequently told me exactly when I was in a situation that put me at risk of people-pleasing, I had just become so used to ignoring it that I never listened to the alarm bells going off. When I felt so dizzy and sick during that lunch with my boss and his wife, my body was telling me loud and clear that working for these people was a situation that had become toxic to my system. The constant symptoms of anxiety I experienced in that office—trembling, shortness of breath, upset stomach, just to name a few—were physical signals my body was using to try to get my attention the entire time.

Working with this new body-centered approach, I now saw that my body regularly gave me exact instructions tailored to specific people and situations. My eyes told me not to make eye contact. My torso told me to turn away from a person. My legs told me to walk away entirely. My hands told me not to type those last two lines of the email offering to do it for them. Of course, the entire time my brain yelled at me that I was being rude and everyone was sure to be angry with me or worse, but the more I listened to my body the less my brain ranted and raved, until most of the time I could hear the quiet yet firm voice of my body above all else.

This sounds like a simple exercise. Let me warn you: it's not. Listening to the body—sometimes in spite of the brain telling you to do the exact opposite—is tough. And when you search for information about people-pleasing and you find a bunch of material telling you that you're codependent and you need to fix that, it's easy to feel like it's all your fault. Now, let me be clear: codependency IS a real thing and it should be addressed if it's a genuine problem in your life. But beyond that, it's important to be aware that critically analyzing a situation to discover if codependency lurks within it is still a mental exercise. It's still using your brain to try to think your way out of the problem.

Moving into the body, in order to better hear the messages of the soul, is an entirely different ball game.

Once you start viewing yourself as a whole, integrated energetic system, you will begin to see that people-pleasing is not just something you are "doing." It is a way of being. And that way of being comes from the way you emotionally feel now, and the way you have emotionally felt in the past, about certain events and outcomes in your life. Once you start shifting the energy of this way of being—by checking into the body, listening to your heart, letting your intuition guide you—boundaries will naturally fall into place much of the time and, for the times you do need to be more forceful, it won't feel like such a struggle.

People-pleasing is a poison, but it's a poison that can be purged out of your system. What comes after is a new sense of self, born out of your own wise body, firmly rooted in your own unique truth.

CHAPTER 5

INFJ Loneliness: How Our Intuition Isolates Us

"How was your weekend?"

It was the question I heard—and hated answering—every Monday morning. Without fail, one of my coworkers was sure to ask how my weekend had been, what I did, etc., and then I would be expected to ask them the same question in return and dutifully listen as they detailed their shopping trip or visit with family.

I'd worked in various offices for over a decade, and by now, I knew the process very well.

After I learned more about being an introvert, my abhorrence of this innocent office ritual suddenly made sense. Introverts dislike small talk. We want to go deeper and connect over issues that are more meaningful than the weather or how a certain football team is doing that year. I totally got this. I *do* hate small talk. But it didn't fully explain my struggle with stunted and unsatisfying communication. Because that struggle didn't only happen with coworkers, acquaintances, and strangers on the bus. At some point, it happened with everyone, even my close friends and people I genuinely liked and looked forward to seeing. It happened with my husband. Sometimes, as weird as this sounds, it even happened with myself.

Whenever anyone asked me how I was or how things were going for me, I just had a really hard time answering that question in any sort of coherent way. Because, inside, in the deepest depths of my soul, where I spend roughly 40 to 70 percent of my time, things were tumultuous. I was always going through something huge, even if nothing seemed to be happening on the outside. If winter was turning into spring I was in the middle of a massive inner rebirth, feeling every subtle nuance of the change in the air and launching into a state of hyper creativity until I was bursting at the seams with new ideas and plans. If fall was turning into winter, I felt myself going more internal each day, a little more immersed in sorrow as I felt the ending of the year approach, anticipating the dark magic of the winter solstice and its unexpected burst of hope as I realized longer days were returning.

If I had a conflict with someone or had been involved in a frustrating conversation or felt like I'd overstepped a boundary, I was in a whirl. I felt my mind and body spinning, caught in an obsessive loop of overthinking and desperate self-soothing attempts that didn't work. And if something big and new happened I froze in place. My introverted intuition downloaded an almost overwhelming flow of information and I simultaneously saw and knew how the rest of the event would unfold, but I was unable to explain this knowledge to anyone else as I could barely put it into words.

These are just a few of the intense emotional states I might go into on any given day and, when I say a few, I really mean just a few. There are dozens of variations. Even when *nothing is happening* I'm usually sunk so deeply into my inner world that I am only half in this one. The other half of me is floating somewhere out in space.

So, this makes communication with other people, at times, extremely difficult.

I do just fine if I'm accessing my extraverted feeling function and asking people questions all about *their* lives. I have no problem empathizing with whatever a person might be going through. I know, too, that this is why I've never had a problem making and keeping a strong circle of friends. People like me because I listen to them and I genuinely care. This is not rocket science.

But, like most INFJs and INFPs, when the tables are turned and it's time for me to share something about myself, I feel blocked. Everything that is most important to me, everything that has any *meaning* to it, comes from my dominant function, my introverted intuition. And explaining my experience with introverted intuition is like trying to hold onto water.

From my discussions with INFPs, I know it's similar for them. Their world revolves almost entirely around introverted feeling, so they go through an intensity of emotion that is almost unimaginable to other people. Like introverted intuition, introverted feeling is incredibly hard to put into words. So, like the INFJ, the INFP tends to experience that same sense of blocked communication whenever they try to truly explain themselves to another person.

For most of my life, this feeling of not being able to explain myself or what was going on with me to other people left me feeling deeply lonely, and with little hope that the situation would ever change.

Another aspect of my introverted intuition that I've found to be difficult is the way it works with my auxiliary function, extraverted feeling. My extraverted feeling has always drawn others to me, and once they're drawn in, they realize they can confide in me. But then, as they tell me their problems, my introverted intuition kicks in so hard I can't help but to share some of the insights it's giving me. In the moment, especially if the person is in crisis and desperately seeking a solution, they're interested in the information. But then, sometimes sooner and sometimes later, another moment comes after that, when the person realizes *how* deeply I can see into them. That's when they get uncomfortable. They begin to regret that they shared so much with me and made themselves so vulnerable. And then I get the cold shoulder the next time we run into each other.

This happened a lot with my dad when I was in my 20s and 30s. My dad was a workaholic surgeon, a very mental guy who lived up in his head most of the time. He also carried a lot of emotional trauma that he suppressed through alcoholism. But every now and again my dad would go through some sort of crisis in his life and he always called me to talk about it. I was always elated and felt like we were finally connecting because he was able to be emotionally vulnerable with me.

Then, like clockwork, he would freeze me out for the next few months and every time I talked to him it was like the crisis conversation had never happened.

One time as we were talking, during one of his stressful periods, my intuition ignited. I started receiving information that I knew was for him. Instead of holding back, I decided to be open about it and let him know exactly what I was seeing about his emotional life. He laughed nervously and then said, "You know, sometimes you tell me things about myself and…they're *true*. I don't know how you know these things, but you do. It's very strange." Then he did that nervous little laugh again and I thought, *oh no, here comes the deep freeze*. And I was right. I didn't hear from him after that for quite a while.

My experience with my dad is something INFJs and INFPs go through with people, on the regular. On one hand, we have a nearly impossible time conveying our true emotional state and inner life to anyone else, and on the other hand, when we do connect deeply with someone, there is a very good chance we might freak that person out with our vision and insight into their soul. The fact that we easily see beyond the mask can cause a great amount of anxiety in others, and it seems that some never fully forgive us for causing them that anxiety.

But, the thing is, *we cannot help it*. We absolutely do not control the way we are wired, the way we were born, or the way we came advantageously equipped into this world to interpret the emotional and soul side of life. We are what we are, and we can't change it. Even if most of us have tried like hell to be anything other than what we really are at one time or another, all of us, on some level, know that there is no getting away from it.

This leaves us lonely, and a lot of the time, also feeling rejected.

In an INFJ or INFP's adolescent and young adult years, it's common for us to choose to reject the world right back. Because by that time it's become obvious to us that "the world" doesn't share our values anyway. We have experienced constant confusion, sometimes despair, because it seems we live on a planet that only values competition, aggression, and an almost exclusively mental approach to life. So why should we continue to participate? Won't it just be the way it's always been for us? We'll be left feeling lost, rejected, ignored, and so very, very lonely.

I believe this is one of the reasons that so many great artists, writers, and other creative visionaries end up depressed and suicidal. When you feel like no one understands you, but at the same time you understand so many people to the core of their soul—*and* your values clash with just about everything else on earth—the outlook can appear pretty grim.

However, I also believe that all this is changing for INFJs and INFPs, due to the internet. Technology has opened up a whole new emotional landscape for just about everyone.

My life changed when I discovered the online introvert awareness movement, and then that I was an INFJ. But after that, I needed more. This interesting label of "INFJ" and the brisk summaries online that told me I was a "counselor," or an "advocate," just weren't enough. So, I searched until I found other INFJs and INFPs. I found them on Facebook, on Twitter, writing various blogs, and, in recent years, self-publishing various books. When I started my own coaching business and began talking to other INFJs and INFPs on the phone on a daily basis, that's when I broke through to an entirely new level.

Once I was in continuous contact with people who were similar in temperament and shared my same values, I felt that I had the social support in place to give me sustenance and strength to go forth and interact in the wider world. Suddenly, I didn't mind so much that extroverts were so…well, extroverted. I was able to soften my attitudes and opinions to give space to others who held different attitudes and opinions. I didn't feel rejected anymore, I didn't feel lonely, so I didn't feel like I needed to fight with the world like I had, in one way or another, for so many years of my life.

When I finally had a safe refuge available to me, filled with other introverted, intuitive people, I felt much braver out in the world, and much more willing to take risks, express myself honestly, and forgive others for not getting it when I was trying to explain my intuitive insights or I told them a little bit more about themselves than they wanted to know.

I didn't need my coworkers or my family members to provide understanding or acceptance for me anymore, and I wasn't feeling constantly frustrated when they couldn't come through on that front. Because I had new friends in my life: sensitive, introverted, intuitive, creative, compassionate, artistic, beautiful friends who understood me at the deepest levels, because they lived in those deep levels too.

If you are an INFJ or an INFP who has felt lonely, misunderstood, and rejected for most of your life, the key to things getting better is the internet, as odd an answer as that might seem. There are *thousands* of INFJs and INFPs out there, and we're speaking up more every day, we're posting more content for you to find every day. All you have to do is look and explore, and then take a risk and reach out.

We will reach right back, I promise.

CHAPTER 6
INFJ Avoidance: Our Favorite Dysfunctional Way of Protecting Ourselves

"Hey Fred. How's it going?"

"Well, not too good. I got some news."

Just from hearing that one little sentence, my stomach began to sink.

Fred was one of my closest friends. I'd known him for 14 years. When we met in 2004 I had only been in San Francisco for less than a month and was working my first job there, at a store that sold running shoes and apparel for triathletes in the Marina District. Fred was part of a running group that met at the store every Wednesday night. After discovering that we shared an interest in Dostoyevsky and Civil War history we became fast friends, despite the fact that we couldn't be more opposite in nature. Fred was a talkative extrovert who loved to be in the thick of things, while I was a sensitive introvert, who much preferred spending quiet time alone.

There was also a bit of an age difference between us. When I met Fred, he was 72 years old and I was 26.

Flash forward 14 years later and here I was on the phone with him. As Fred was now 86 years old, when he said he "got some news" I knew it probably wasn't good.

Very calmly, he went on to tell me that it looked like he might have cancer. He still needed to have some tests done, and his doctors said that if he did have it, this particular type was so slow moving that he would probably come to the end of his life naturally before he began to suffer from the more severe effects of the disease. Since Fred was 86 years old, it might seem safe to assume that he was a frail elderly person calling me from an assisted living facility, but nothing could be further from the truth. Fred still walked three miles a day, every day. He weight-trained at the gym. He had just self-published a book on Abraham Lincoln and was constantly busy with speaking engagements and book tours that he organized—start-to-finish—himself. On his odd days off, he was down at City Hall, advocating for the rights of the mentally ill and homeless.

In a word, Fred was a powerhouse.

So, I never imagined Fred dying, not really. I kind of always thought he might outlive me.

When I heard Fred might have cancer I tried to fight off the tears. But what really gutted me was what he said next. "I'd like to see you soon, if you can fit me into your schedule. You're a very special friend to me, even if you do disappear for long periods of time."

If you can fit me into your schedule.

Even if you do disappear…for long periods of time.

Those words knifed me in the heart, not only because I knew they were true, but because they implied so much about the way I handled relationships.

Hi, I'm Lauren. And I'm avoidant with a capital "A."

For a long time, I assumed I was avoidant because of my childhood. While that's definitely part of it, the more I've studied the INFJ personality type and the more I've gotten to know other INFJs in real life, the more I've seen that avoidance is not just a strategy that was borne out of my past experiences with trauma. If we get to choose our types of dysfunction, avoidance is a very INFJ choice to make. I saw this clearly as I talked to other INFJs about their own emotional patterns. It could not be a coincidence that almost all of us follow the same pattern when threatened or hurt: Retreat, withdraw, and then avoid. And then avoid some more.

For me, avoidance was such a go-to mechanism that I couldn't imagine my life without it. After a bad breakup right after college I jumped into a series of romantic relationships, and ended them all before they could go anywhere. I quit jobs and moved cities like I was sampling different Starbucks locations. All of my friends—*all* of them—said the same things to me. *We never see you. It would be nice if you called more. You're always busy.*

I never called someone first. I found it difficult to set aside time for loved ones. I found it impossible to express to someone that my feelings had been hurt or that I needed help or something else from them. And, for the longest time, I never saw anything wrong with that.

It just seemed that I didn't need people as much as others did. Most people felt clingy to me, even if I loved them and even if I understood why. I chalked that up to me being weird and abnormal, which had become a catch-all category long ago for all the ways that I had observed I was different from the rest of the population.

But when I started diving deep into what makes an INFJ an INFJ, that's when I saw the pattern. It wasn't just me. A lot of us—an overwhelming amount of us—are avoidant. Two of the big ways it seems to manifest is either in perfectionism and workaholism, or self-destructiveness and addiction. Both ways take over our time, attention, and energy until there is none left for our families or friends or anyone new. Both keep us feeling safe and function as a self-soothing strategy.

Both lead only to despair and disaster at the very end. Always.

So, why are so many INFJs avoidant?

The most obvious answer, to me, is that most INFJs and INFPs learn from a young age that we are different, and that our difference is not good. Other people don't like it and let the INFJ or INFP know they don't like it. Because INFJs and INFPs are so incredibly sensitive, this feels tantamount to a rejection of our whole being, our entire worth as a human.

Many INFJs and INFPs also have an intense reaction to our first heartbreak. It's not something we "get over" and move through relatively quickly, as other adolescents seem to do. First love for an INFJ or INFP seems to be the equivalent of a war experience. Many of us come out of it completely traumatized, without even the words to describe what we're experiencing. On top of that, we're usually surrounded by other teenagers or parents who are very different in temperament from us, so when we try to find support or communicate the way our trampled hearts feel, it's not uncommon for us to be told that we're exaggerating or obsessing too much.

There may be other experiences that play out similarly for INFJs and INFPs. The situation itself is not important. What is important is that something happens for us, something big that feels like an earth-shattering event, something that shakes our very soul. But when we try to reach out to communicate this feeling to someone else, when we try to tell someone, "my soul has been shaken," we are met with uncomprehending looks, mockery, or plain confusion. Then we feel rejected on the deepest levels.

That's when we start to retreat, and shortly after, to withdraw.

Once we have withdrawn all the way into our shells to lick our wounds, we find that it's not so bad in there. Actually, it's kind of cozy. This protected, fortressed inner space isn't *that* different from being in our bedroom with the door locked and a pile of books. It's nice in there. There aren't any other people to deal with. We don't have to handle trying to manage another person's emotions externally while also trying to process them internally. We don't have to face rejection. We don't have to struggle with the reaction everyone else seems to have to our weird selves. *We just don't have to deal with any of it.*

And wow, *that* feels kind of nice.

Sometimes it's healthy to pull into this guarded inner space and be a turtle for a while to recuperate from trauma, large and small. As INFJs and INFPs are, of course, introverts, this means we genuinely enjoy spending time alone, and because we're used to not very many other people understanding us, we know how to spend time alone in countless different ways, all of them fun. It's when we turn a certain corner, when we decide that maybe we'll just live from now on with part of ourselves—a significant part—*always* in this guarded, secret place, that we run into real trouble. Because retreat and withdrawal come so naturally to our temperament, after that, sustained avoidance is easy. Then we get stuck there.

Once we're stuck, there's only one way out. And it's not easy. In fact, it's probably one of the hardest things to do in this day and age.

We have to open our hearts, and we have to embrace being uncomfortable.

We have to bring down our shields, let down our guard, and actually (gasp!) invite people in. We need to push ourselves, just the tiniest bit, to initiate communication and take risks in connecting with others. We need to try being vulnerable, not with everyone and not all the time, but definitely sometimes, when we feel like it might be safe and it could be helpful.

If you're like most INFJs you probably already have a small, close circle of friends. After all, we are very, very good with people. I'm not suggesting that our avoidance strategies lead us to be completely closed-off hermits. But look at your circle and ask yourself: *How open am I? How open am I really?*

When was the last time you honestly told someone when your feelings were hurt by something that happened between the two of you? When was the last time that you admitted to yourself how deeply your anger or embarrassment over a past situation went?

If you're looking at these questions and cringing, or even just nodding and seeing yourself in them, then you're not alone. You're just a normal introverted intuitive feeler.

There's nothing wrong with our tendency to go into retreat/withdrawal mode as a response to trauma, and there's nothing wrong with our avoidant tendencies either. But it's all a question of balance. Once we go too far with avoidance, our relationships begin to suffer and we end up experiencing a lot less joy in life.

The people who love us end up experiencing a lot less joy, too.

I realized all of this and more during that phone call with my friend Fred, who did have cancer as it turned out. At that time, I needed Fred's diagnosis to serve as a wake-up call. I needed the reminder of how much he meant to me, and also the reminder that our lifetimes are not infinite and time with our loved ones is limited. After that experience I approached my relationships differently. Instead of packing my to-do list with too many activities, I scheduled in big chunks of free time filled with nothing, waiting there on my calendar to nurture me with space or to be filled with friends and family. I slowed down and made it a point to call people, even if I kept it relatively brief because I'm not too keen about talking on the phone.

Maybe most importantly, I reordered my priorities. I put myself first, my loved ones immediately after that, and work and projects third. The avoidant workaholic in me was not happy about this, but my overall happiness level went up so much I found I didn't care. And, after a while, my workaholic self stopped grumbling when she saw it was pointless to fight the change.

If you're an avoidant INFJ or INFP, making the choice to turn and face whatever it is you're running from—or slowing down and letting life unfold naturally—could be the choice that changes your life.

I know it changed mine.

CHAPTER 7

The Empath and the Narcissist: Finding the Link Between the Unicorn and the Harpy

When I was a little girl my favorite movie on earth was The Last Unicorn. It's an animated film from 1982, based on the book by Peter S. Beagle, and populated with famous voices like Jeff Bridges and Mia Farrow. For those of you who haven't seen it, the title pretty much says it all. It's about a unicorn who is the last unicorn in the world. She leaves her safe forest to go on an adventurous journey to a dark castle at the edge of the land, where it's rumored she'll meet the evil Red Bull, who is apparently keeping all the other unicorns captive.

This sounds like the makings for a cheesy movie, but to my child self, it was anything but that. The Last Unicorn touched something deep inside me. It spoke to some hidden reservoir of emotion in my heart that possibly I hadn't even been aware of before seeing the film. I would also bet that I wasn't the only child who had that reaction to it. As an adult, I attended a screening of The Last Unicorn at the historic Castro Theater in San Francisco in 2013, hosted by Peter S. Beagle himself, and tickets were sold out, with people crowding into the back in the standing-room-only section. I wasn't the only one who was sniffling when the opening credits began to roll.

As I looked around the audience, I realized everyone else there was just like me. Eccentric, creative, introverted, bookish…weird. People who had always felt like freaks in comparison to the rest of the general population. I wasn't the only one who had connected so strongly with the character of a lone unicorn, the only one of her kind in the world, who had been alone for so long she didn't even realize she was lonely anymore. I wasn't the only one who felt like I was maybe something special that no one else could see.

There is another part of the movie that resonates very deeply with me as well, although I didn't understand why for the longest time. As the unicorn forges onward in her journey, she's captured by Mommy Fortuna, an old crone with a traveling circus show of mythical oddities, including a manticore and a minotaur, among others. Most of the "mythical creatures" are weak, but normal, animals that Mommy Fortuna has enchanted so that observers see something fantastic. The manticore is really an old lame lion and the minotaur is actually an injured monkey. But in addition to the unicorn, Mommy Fortuna does have one other genuine article in her collection: a harpy. She tells the unicorn that the harpy is the real thing and it was only luck that allowed her to capture her. The harpy had been asleep when Mommy Fortuna stumbled upon her.

Well, of course, the unicorn escapes, but as she's breaking out of Mommy Fortuna's weird zoo, she goes around and sets all the other animals free too. And then she comes to the harpy's cage. She seems to hesitate for a moment—and the viewer is hesitating too, we know that if she lets that harpy out there's a good chance the harpy will immediately kill her—but then she looks into the harpy's eyes and the harpy says to her, "Set me free. We are sisters, you and I." And the unicorn lowers her horn and burns the lock off the harpy's cage.

"We are sisters, you and I."

Something about that line pierced my eight-year-old heart. Although, at the time, I had no idea why.

Flash forward 20 years later. It was 2007 and I was working for my first startup. I had gotten the job through the writing program I attended at the time. The writing program and the startup were owned and run by the same woman and in the matter of a few short months this woman had become my mentor, teacher, and idol. She seemed to be everything I wanted to be—independent, intelligent, charismatic, sophisticated, and a brilliant writer and entrepreneur. It wasn't until I had gotten in deep with her that I began to see what she really was.

There had been warning signs from the very beginning, but I had blown past them all like I was crazy drunk and blowing through stop signs. She had a quick-change personality and could go from gushing euphoric praise to viciously cold disapproval in a matter of seconds. She was a perfectionist in everything and threw tantrums over the tiniest of mistakes. After I started working at her startup I started catching her in lies, big ones. And then began the real game: constant, cruel manipulation.

After just a few months of working for her I had radically changed. I had dropped weight and had dark circles under my eyes. I was always exhausted but suffered from insomnia. I was worried every second of every day that I would make a mistake and incur her wrath. Almost all my energy went toward anticipating her needs and demands. I felt like I was plugged in to her and she was feeding off me and I couldn't unplug myself, I couldn't yank the cord out of the socket and set myself free. And I had no idea why.

Finally, I hit a breaking point. I was having panic attacks daily and realized that if I didn't quit that job I might very well have some sort of nervous breakdown. It took me months, if not years, to heal from the experience, and almost the same amount of time to figure out what had even happened in that situation.

I had been trapped in the clutches of a narcissist.

The term "narcissist" gets tossed around frequently these days, and while I'm glad the phenomenon is getting more exposure, I have also observed that the definition of what constitutes a narcissist in most people's minds is really just a person with a big ego who is relatively vain and self-absorbed. These traits can be annoying to deal with, but they don't come close to actual narcissism.

In my experience with my toxic boss, things between us escalated very rapidly. I was immediately attracted to her when I joined the writing program. Her energy felt so compelling. On her end, she seemed to zero in on me a little more each time we met. When I started working for her, our dynamic easily fell into a dysfunctional routine. Establishing a codependent attachment with each other took place so smoothly I had no idea it was even happening. What I did notice was that she got tired of everyone, quickly, everyone except me. Sooner or later, whoever surrounded her was fired or villainized or worse, everyone except me. It seemed I was one of the only people on earth who knew how to please her.

I was dependent on my toxic boss, like a drug. And, like a drug, even after I realized how harmful she was, I had a hell of a time letting her go.

This experience impacted me so powerfully that I ended up writing all about it in my second autobiographical novel, *West Is San Francisco.* In that book, I laid out every detail of our sick relationship and how it spiraled out of control so fast. I also examined why we were so attracted to each other. As I was unraveling the threads of my story it had bothered me to no end. Why had I been so drawn to a narcissist in the first place? Why had I let her in? It wasn't until a few years later that I found the answer, the other piece of the puzzle that seemed to be missing for so long.

I was an empath.

I was an empath and she was a narcissist, and the two went together like night and day. Or, like a unicorn and a harpy.

We are sisters, you and I.

Sisters…yeah. Something about that felt very right and true to me.

So, I started researching the connection between empaths and narcissists online, and what I found wasn't very surprising. Empaths and narcissists are naturally drawn to each other, experts say, for a variety of reasons. Empaths want to preserve harmony no matter the cost, so they will let a narcissist run roughshod over their boundaries. Also, in the empath the narcissist finds a seemingly bottomless reservoir of compassion, understanding, forgiveness, and desire to please. The narcissist has an almost preternatural instinct for sniffing out those who have an extraordinary capacity to give, because they have an extraordinary capacity to take.

Once a narcissist-empath relationship is established the empath just keeps giving and giving and giving, pretty much until their system burns out and they go into total collapse. Because the narcissist is a born taker and the empath a born giver, it's easy for the two to form a perfect symbiotic relationship with each other. Perfect, except for the fact that it usually destroys the empath and razes their emotional center to the ground, just to name one of the teeny-tiny little side effects.

Educating myself on the research helped, but just partly. Because there was still another dynamic at play that I couldn't quite put my finger on, not until I finished the novel I already mentioned, *West Is San Francisco.* As I wrote the closing scenes of the book I finally realized what had made things click so perfectly between me and my toxic boss.

She was a sensitive intuitive person, just like me.

Now, maybe she wasn't an INFJ, I couldn't be sure of that. But she was *some* sort of intuitive, I was willing to bet my life. It was her sharp intuitive skills that allowed her to so effortlessly feel out the weak spots, the vulnerabilities and trigger points, in others. It was her intuitive side that warned her when she was about to get caught in too many lies and helped her keep a safe course with her constant thirst for manipulation. It was her intuitive skills that fueled her incredible charisma, and brought more people into her inner circle whenever she needed more warm bodies from which to siphon her energy.

The more I thought about it, the more I became convinced of it. My toxic boss had once been a sensitive intuitive person, just like me. But something had happened to her, something deep in her past, and that something had turned her into the ruthless narcissist she was in the present day. I couldn't be sure of the exact trauma, but I felt instinctively that after that traumatic event my boss had come to an emotional crossroads where she needed to make a choice: Attempt to heal and seek the light, or shut down totally and throw her lot in with the dark.

She chose to go to the dark side.

I remain convinced of this theory today—that narcissists used to be empaths when they were on the light side, and so now, living on the dark side, they consciously and unconsciously return to that population to use it as a feeding ground. I have also seen my theory borne out again and again through stories and accounts from other INFJs and INFPs, my clients and the friends I've made online. It's so common for us to go through at least one big relationship with a narcissist in our lives that it seems almost like a textbook requirement for being a sensitive intuitive person.

I think that's really the truth of the matter. It's not just that empaths and narcissists have a symbiotic relationship. Instead, when empaths and narcissists come together, for both of them, it's like looking into a mirror. Each one gazes back at the other, thinking about the choices they've made, fascinated by what they could have become.

CHAPTER 8
INFJs and Narcissistic Abuse: Forcing Ourselves into a Choice about Power

If the theory I put forth in the previous chapter is correct, and narcissists start out in life as INFJs or INFPs (who are almost always empaths) and then choose to self-actualize through their dark side instead of the light, then it's understandable why empaths and narcissists are attracted to each other, especially when we take into account the empath's propensity toward helping others to heal.

But what's in it for the empathic INFJ or INFP working on the light side? The narcissist gets boatloads of compassion and forgiveness and healing energy from us, but it appears that we get nothing but pain and grief.

When I came out of the relationship with my toxic boss I felt so traumatized and damaged that I had to take three months off work completely. When I tried to explain what had happened to other people, no one understood except for my husband, who is a Highly Sensitive Person himself, and an INTJ personality type. All my other friends told me I was blowing things out of proportion and being melodramatic about the situation.

For a long time afterward, I thought I had gained nothing from the experience of getting wrapped up with a narcissist. I felt like a total victim. Like I had just been wandering along, minding my own business, when I fell into her web-like trap. I became convinced that what had happened only proved how weak and stupid I was, how oblivious I could be to the ill intentions of others. In short, I spent quite a while feeling like complete shit.

It wasn't until I began writing about my experience that I could begin to make sense of it. After I wrote the story into what ultimately became the form of an autobiographical novel, I was able to see the big picture.

That's when I pieced together the pattern and found the meaning behind what had initially seemed like totally random events.

The truth was, I did gain something from my experience with my toxic boss: empowerment. Even though I hadn't felt very strong at the time, and I criticized myself afterward for keeping my feelings bottled up while I was working for her, and then quitting the job with as little fireworks as possible, I realized later that the situation had forced me to take care of myself in a radical way. Me quitting that job wasn't a weak move, it was the most loving thing I could have done for myself. And me keeping my real feelings hidden from the narcissist who was abusing me wasn't an action borne solely out of fear, but also out of an instinct of self-preservation, because if I had ever told her how I really felt, she would only have gone into war mode and attacked me mercilessly, damaging my psyche even further.

As I wrote about my experiences, and then formed those experiences into a narrative with a theme and a story arc, and characters and symbols, I began to see how my relationship with my toxic boss had pushed me to grow and evolve, albeit in a very extreme way.

Up until that point in my life, I had spent years giving my power away to other people. I was an expert in people-pleasing, and in side-stepping my own wants and needs so that someone else could come before me. I hardly ever shared my real feelings with *anyone*, and my self-worth had been in the toilet since my teenage years. It was immensely difficult for me to speak up, listen to my own inner signals, and take care of myself, even when my body and the state of my health screamed at me that I was on the brink of mental and/or physical crisis.

If I hadn't met my toxic boss, who pushed me so far to the wall, it's very likely I could have spent *decades* like this, continuing to rely on my people-pleasing skills to get by in most situations and slowly being eaten alive on the inside from festering resentment and anger. The relationship I had with my toxic boss ripped away my illusions and showed me exactly what would happen if I kept on the path I was going down, and because I chose a narcissist to be my teacher she was able to show me the information I needed over a period of eight months, instead of eight years.

After I saw the big picture, I stopped feeling like a victim. I knew now that something in me had subconsciously chosen this experience with my narcissist, and I had chosen it because I was ready to upgrade my life.

In my opinion, this is the key to understanding the complicated relationship that can occur between INFJs or INFPs and narcissists. The only way out of the prison of the abusive narcissistic relationship is for us to step into our own power, instead of choosing the path of the eternal victim. Yes, narcissists are abusers, for sure, but in adult relationships in which both parties are there of their own free will *no one can continue to abuse us unless we give them permission to do so*. What the narcissist does, at a very extreme level for the INFJ or INFP, is to show up and demand that we either give or deny them permission.

Now, this doesn't mean that we will be successful at stepping into our own power on the first go-round with a narcissist. My toxic boss was not the first narcissist to wander into my life. Before her, I had a history of involvement with toxic people, of varying shades of negativity and malignancy. But my toxic boss *was* the first narcissist with whom I chose to draw such a firm boundary. When I left her, I never went back. I never let her reenter my life. Then, instead of immediately finding a new toxic relationship, as I had so many times in the past, I used writing to make sense of my experience, and to learn from it.

I'm not saying that leaving a narcissistic relationship is easy, and I'm not saying that getting involved with a narcissist is anyone's fault either. I don't believe in playing the blame game. I believe instead that all of us are on our own path and we make thousands of conscious and subconscious choices over a lifetime to travel further down that path. There are no "wrong moves." There is only the next move. What I am saying, though, is that if you are an INFJ or an INFP who has found yourself in a relationship with a narcissistic abuser, what you've been given is an opportunity.

With every narcissist, we have the opportunity to do a deep dive into learning about boundaries. Some narcissists are physically abusive, which brings up the most primal of boundary issues. How do we expect other people to treat our bodies? What is acceptable and what is absolutely not? Other narcissists focus more on emotional and mental manipulation, which brings up a different kind of boundary issue. Who do we grant access to our heart and to our mind? Does anyone else get to dictate our belief systems to us? Still other narcissists lie, cheat, steal, and engage in other forms of betrayal. Again, boundary issues.

In everyday life personal boundaries run the risk of coming across as vague, confusing, or easily misunderstood by the parties involved. The interesting thing about narcissists is that—after you see past their standard smoke-and-mirrors routine—they make our boundary issues crystal clear. If you struggle with holding boundaries around your body or your mind, or the physical and/or emotional structures of your life, a narcissist will make that very apparent to you, very quickly. They cut through a lot of psychological red tape in an extremely short period of time.

It's common for boundary issues to be an area that is unparalleled in intensity for INFJs and INFPs. Because we are so energetically sensitive, and empathic in a variety of ways, our sense of where we end and others begin is usually hazy from a very young age. It doesn't come naturally to us to defend our space and hold firm boundaries with other people. This is something we have to learn, and as shitty as the experience can be with one of them, a narcissist can also be one of our greatest teachers in this department.

If you've recently gone through an experience with a narcissist and everything you're reading here is stabbing even deeper into the wound,

I get that. It's okay if this doesn't resonate with you. For a full two to three years after my experience with my toxic boss I just could not get on board with the idea that she was possibly one of my greatest teachers. I wanted her to suffer for how she had acted with me and my coworkers, or at least have the self-awareness to see how negatively her behavior affected other people. As I've said, it wasn't until I was able to process my experience by turning it into story that I began to see the gifts the experience had given me. If you're not there yet, it's okay. And if you never get there, that's cool too. Everyone has a different experience. My story is just one way to look at things.

The last important thing to know is that narcissists are not people to be feared, especially if we've used our experiences to empower ourselves with secure and reasonable boundaries. I talk to so many INFJs and INFPs who have been through a relationship with a narcissistic abuser and are now terrified of ever running across another one. The fear this engenders keeps the INFJ or the INFP from ever fully opening up again. They become suspicious of everyone. They always wonder if their relationships are too one-sided or if the person is "just using them." Don't get me wrong, it can be helpful to evaluate your relationships periodically. If you feel that the other party is more of a taker than a giver, it's okay to cut them loose and not feel badly about it. But that doesn't mean that you should never trust anyone again. Holding onto your fear that the narcissists are out there and waiting to pounce isn't going to improve your life in any way.

Instead, it's most helpful to consistently remind yourself that *you* hold the power in your life. *You* make your own choices and *you* decide who stays and who goes. *You* decide your boundaries, and if someone else doesn't respect them, then *you* have the right to kick them out of your life, no explanation needed.

Yes, going through a relationship with a narcissist is a special kind of hell all its own that seems to be especially reserved for empathic personality types, but I believe that there is a good reason behind it. It just takes patience, persistence, and acceptance to find the jewels hidden among the thorns.

Fortunately, INFJs and INFPs are people who tend to have these qualities in abundance.

PART II

RISING UP:

Taking Our INFJ Power Back

CHAPTER 1

The INFJ Emotional Center: Stepping into Our Primary Power Source

"I don't know what's wrong with me, or why I can't get this project done. I had such great ideas…in the beginning. And then I submitted them all to my professor, and the committee, and they gave me good feedback but…it was hard to stick to the outline they suggested. So I made a list of goals, but I haven't been able to meet any of those either, and every time I look at the outline or the goals list now, I just feel…depressed. And tired. Like a failure."

I was on the phone with a new client and she was close to tears. She'd shared with me how she had joined a particular graduate program because they had seemed to offer everything she wanted, and she felt sure the program would be just what she needed to produce the book she'd been dreaming of writing for so long. The book was only going to be a starting point though, she told me. She wanted to expand into teaching workshops and offering online courses and also blogging. She wanted to create her own program out of all these elements, a program that was built for women who wanted to reignite their creativity and use it to help the world.

She'd had very high hopes for the graduate program, she said. She'd thought the academic setting would help her get into gear and meet deadlines on writing her book, and also provide the support system she needed to move forward after that. But now she felt shut down, exhausted, and like all her good ideas had dried up. She felt like she was doing everything wrong, but she didn't know how to make it right.

Fortunately, I had seen this exact scenario many times before, and the solution was easier, and more obvious, than my new client thought.

As happens so much of the time in my coaching sessions, the problem was not what the client thought the problem was. This client thought the problem was that she couldn't stick to the outline her professor had suggested, she couldn't meet the deadlines imposed by the committee, and she couldn't achieve the goals on her goal list. She was "doing everything all wrong," as she said. Well, she *was* taking the wrong approach, but not in the way she assumed. The problem wasn't that she couldn't achieve the objectives, the problem was that she was trying to produce things by accessing energy from her weakest areas.

As I considered how I could help this client I was brought back to the work of Jose and Lena Stevens, shamanic teachers, practitioners, and also professional consultants who advocate a shamanic approach to the way people build and sustain their businesses. When I discovered Jose and Lena a few years ago they changed the way I saw everything.

Jose and Lena teach that there are three main centers that humans work from: intellectual, emotional, and physical. Every person works primarily from one center, most of the time, but also shifts between centers as needed. So, someone who is intellectually-centered tends to be measured and rational in their approach to life. Someone who is physically-centered is more grounded in their body and more comfortable with the visual, the sensual, and anything movement oriented. Those who are emotionally-centered live through their hearts. They "feel" their way through life and can tune into emotions with little problem.

INFJs are, maybe not so obviously, emotionally-centered. Why "not so obviously"? Because we have strong organizational skills, and being so future oriented, we are born planners. Due to our exceptional ability to create and follow systems, and keep the files in order, we can come across as thinkers surprisingly often. However, at the core, we are feelers. We operate *primarily* from an emotional vantage point. When we take in the world, we run it through our emotional filter first. So, no matter what we look like on the surface, this doesn't change the fact that we are deeply emotional beings and extremely sensitive, whether we like it or not.

The INFJ's auxiliary function is *extraverted* feeling, one of the main reasons we are so brilliant at ferreting out and addressing the emotions of others. However, *introverted* feeling is one of our shadow functions, which means that sometimes we're not so hot at recognizing and identifying our own emotions, or dealing with them. In addition to this, INFJs are empaths, so we tend to experience and absorb the emotions of the people around us. The last piece of this convoluted puzzle is introverted intuition, our primary function, the most powerful tool in our toolbox, and also a function that needs time to identify and categorize the patterns we use in order to figure out our own emotional landscape. When we put all these elements together it's easy to see why many INFJs end up routinely drowning in emotional confusion.

That's when we flee the scene, and our main escape of choice is almost always our own head.

Escaping into our own mind feels like a very natural choice to the INFJ. Introverted thinking is our tertiary function, so it's something we're halfway decent at if we've matured in life, and it can also be used as a calming agent when we're too overwhelmed by the world, or so stressed that we've temporarily burned out our introverted intuition and extraverted feeling. Introverted thinking can be helpful for INFJs, in moderation, but we will always need to return again to our intuition and our emotional center to access our true source of power.

It's also important to remember that, no matter if we are individuals who are emotionally-centered or physically-centered, all of us live in a culture that is intellectually-centered. This means that our workplaces, our school systems, and any collective social programming are all intellectually-centered. So, in order to fit in and "do well" in this sort of society, one must adopt the intellectual center more often than not, no matter what our real preferred center may be.

Because introverted thinking is a tertiary function for INFJs, and we use the intellectual center as an escape much of the time anyway, we usually blend in to society seamlessly. We do well in school and we do well in the workplace. We can adapt to existing organizational models (even if we would truly rather be creating new ones) and we can follow along with any rational line of thinking quite easily. But just because we blend in like chameleons doesn't mean this is the way we thrive. If we work from the intellectual center too much of the time, and neglect our true center, the emotional center, we will suffer for it, deeply.

This was the real problem my new client was having. Her inspiration, her drive and motivation, her big idea, were all connected to her emotional center. She wanted to help women just like herself. Women who had lost touch with their own creativity and felt the pain of that. She wanted to do healing work with these women and she wanted to do it using her own creative gifts—writing, teaching, and speaking. If she had remained working *primarily* from her emotional center, and used the intellectual and physical centers *as needed,* she probably wouldn't have hit the dead ends she was running into at every turn. She would have had so much energy and creativity available to her that she wouldn't have needed a goals list to worry over.

Because we live in an intellectually-centered society, when INFJs or INFPs seek help for problems like depression, lack of motivation, procrastination, overwhelm, or confusion about their life purpose, the solutions offered up are well-meaning but, again, intellectually-centered. It made perfect sense to my client's professor and committee that what she needed was an outline, deadlines in place, and a goals list. Those things *would* make sense to the intellectually-centered crowd. For an intellectually-centered person, outlines, deadlines, and goals provide comfortable structure and reliable support through any work process. But for a highly creative, emotionally-centered person, when the majority of the creative process is divided into outlines, deadlines, and goals, it can feel stifling and too rigid, even suffocating.

INFJs and INFPs both suffer from the issues outlined above, but in different ways. So, as discussed, we see the INFJ taking refuge in the thinking process, and then pushing it so far that we try to substitute intellect for emotion, our main power source. The INFP, on the other hand, can't get away from the emotional center that easily. For INFPs, introverted feeling is their dominant function. They can't just dissociate themselves from it. When they flee into their heads, instead of getting lost in rational thinking, they more likely get caught in an emotional sea that quickly turns into an emotional storm.

INFPs in this type of situation find it extremely difficult to pull themselves out of it, precisely because they are surrounded by a society that does not fit their needs, on nearly every level. The surrounding culture tells INFPs they should be thinking their way out of their problems and using logic to address the situations in their life. This is like telling a whale that it should learn how to do tricks like a dog because it would go so much better for them if they lived inside and could depend on a bowl of kibble every day. Like whales, INFPs live in the deeps and they have a special, beautiful language all their own. A language that is so beautiful, in fact, it affects other species whenever they hear it, uplifting everyone around them when they speak from the heart.

Of course, the language of the INFP is emotional, through and through. So, when they try to force themselves to operate most frequently from the intellectual center, it's like their very language has been taken away from them and they're forced to speak in the tongue of their oppressors. This might sound dramatic, but I've talked to enough INFPs that I can tell you most of them at one time or another have felt exactly this degree of alienated from mainstream society.

For the INFJ and the INFP, there is only one solution that works effectively: We must use our emotional center as our primary power source. This is not an easy thing to do. It requires us to say no and draw boundaries and turn down or turn away from many things urged upon us by the surrounding culture. It might mean that we have to tell our professor that outlines don't work for us. It might mean that we leave the corporate job (the one we hate anyway) because we cannot stomach adapting to the organizational model already in place and we go off to create our own, even if no one else believes we can do it. It might mean that we become more honest with the people around us in our day-to-day lives, and we own the fact that we work from an emotional center and there is no shame in that.

It could mean speaking up for ourselves more.

It could mean taking more emotional risks.

It will definitely mean being willing to look at the world with new eyes.

Once we begin to routinely access our true power source, our emotional center, we will also begin to speak our special, beautiful language again.

That's when we will be able to communicate with each other and the world, on our terms.

CHAPTER 2
INFJs as Crazy Artists: The Power Behind the Instability of the Creative Mind

"What are you doing this weekend? Any fun plans for tonight?"

It was a normal Friday evening at the office and I was getting ready to head out. I'd stopped by my manager's office to say good night and his questions had caught me off guard. I stopped and stared at him, trying to soften the intense thinking face I seemed to have no power to control whenever someone asked me something, as I desperately tried to formulate an answer that wouldn't sound too weird.

Because, the truth was, I did have fun plans that night. But they were also very strange plans. I was quite sure someone normal would not understand.

The week prior I had been immersed in an extremely creative period. I'd been waking up every day with new ideas for the book I was writing and feeling that slightly manic high that always seemed to possess me whenever I got really wrapped up in one of my stories. Music was a tool I frequently used to connect even more deeply with the well of creativity, and it wasn't uncommon for me to become obsessed with a certain song or set of songs that spoke to the mood I was feeling and the tone of my current creative work.

On this particular evening, my plan had been to go home, lay on the floor for an hour listening to the same song over and over again, and then spend the next hour pacing and snapping my fingers while alternating the first song with one or two others, all of them played over and over again, until I went into something like a creative trance and the ideas started to flow. Then I would scribble down notes for the writing I intended to do the next day, eat a huge meal, and fall into bed exhausted.

This was my idea of a perfect night. When my creativity was peaking I wanted nothing more than to lose myself in my own inner world. The promise of carrying back creative jewels from that world, in order to write about them in this one, gave me a euphoric high that felt better than any drug.

Could I tell my manager this, though? He seemed to be a cool guy, and he also seemed to be genuinely interested in me as a person. Maybe I could…

15 minutes later I left the office with my cheeks burning, feeling that familiar cringing embarrassment and beating myself up. Why-oh-why-oh-*why* had I tried to honestly explain myself to a normal person?

My manager hadn't laughed at me. But he had given me *the look*. As I stumbled through my explanations of how I needed to lay down and then pace and snap as I listened to the same song approximately 76 times in a row, his face had gone from slightly puzzled to seriously confused. When I tried to describe how these activities were the most helpful to me when I was trying to bring something out of the inchoate churning mass of my soul and into the light of day, he only looked more bewildered. Then I tried to backpedal and nervously laughed and shrugged like maybe I had only been kidding about all of it, scurrying away from him as fast as possible.

He probably thinks I'm crazy, I thought, sitting on the bus on the way home and feeling that old familiar pain point come up again. Of course, I knew exactly why it was so painful. Because much of the time I thought I might be crazy too.

For most of my life I had on-and-off doubted my sanity. I never felt like I might harm myself or others—at least, not after I got sober—but I did do things that were just downright odd. Like, listening to the same song on repeat a ridiculous number of times. Also, there was the way I paced and snapped my fingers while working out creative ideas, and the way I talked to fictional characters, sometimes out loud. And sometimes, when I was in a state of what I thought of as, "peak creativity," I *felt* unstable. I swung from one emotional extreme to another. My mind was all over the place. I would be manic and then, a few hours later, depressed and lethargic. According to mainstream opinion, I had more than a few signs of some kind of mood disorder.

Except, deep in my gut, way down deep, I didn't feel like there was anything wrong with me. I had a hunch that the periods of instability were connected to my periods of creativity. They seemed to always go together, and it had to be more than a coincidence.

When I started coaching writers five years later, I got confirmation that my hunch was correct.

Almost every INFJ or INFP I coached reported the same thing I experienced: periods of intense creativity accompanied by feelings of mental and emotional instability. My clients talked about all the things I went through: mood swings, mania and depression, even listening to the same song over and over (which definitely seems to be an INFJ thing, in particular). Also, and maybe most importantly, they talked about doubting their own sanity and how nervous and scared that made them feel.

So, I wasn't alone. That made me feel better all by itself. But, I was still intrigued. As a writer, I was familiar with the stories of crazy artists. Stories about writers and poets who suffered from alcoholism or drug abuse, struggled with mental illness, and ended up committing suicide seemed to be a dime a dozen. As an INFJ, of course I had to ask: What was the underlying pattern?

Then I got into shamanism and started learning about energetic patterns and realized that the theory of creativity and instability going hand-in-hand is not only already well known in the realm of shamanic studies, but it's not always seen as a negative thing like it is in so much of Western culture.

Shamans know that creativity *needs* a certain level of instability to thrive. However, from what I've observed, we live in a society that is extremely uncomfortable with uncertainty (which is just another form of instability), and so most of us are impatient to get things nailed down and shoved into a familiar box as soon as possible. When we try to nail down and categorize creativity before it's even had time to give birth to a new work of art or a new idea, the creative impulse fizzles and dies. Creativity is not something that can be controlled, and it balks at having to stick to a plan.

The only environment in which creativity can truly blossom is an unstable environment. When instability comes into play, everything loosens up. This is cool, because creativity needs a lot of big open space in which to expand. Pure creativity is like a child who only wants to dance. Arms and legs might flail around clumsily, the movements are made up as they go along, and the dance can change in the blink of an eye if a different song begins to play. No matter what the dance looks like, the energy of it is the same. The child dances out of love for the music, and the desire to move in response to that love.

Within the energy of instability, most of the possibilities are still available to us. Things might keep growing, or they could collapse. There is room for new people and events to show up in our lives, and a bigger field of options in which to play. Literally, *anything could happen*. Obviously, this can feel scary to a lot of people.

This is also, incidentally, one of the main reasons so many writers feel so uncomfortable while writing the first draft of their book. Even when using an outline, a sloppy first draft still might zig when the writer expected it to zag. That's why it's important to be mindful of how essential a certain level of instability is to creative work. Because when writers panic and try to buckle down and get rigid about expectations for their stories, creativity tends to depart without so much as a backward glance.

Of course, rigidity is not all bad. There is always a time and place for structure. Without set plans and organized structures, society would go haywire. We live on a planet chock full of people, and with the world population exploding more each day, we need certain structures more than ever. Chaos plus seven billion people on one little earth is a recipe for disaster.

It's when we begin to depend too much on structure and expect it to show up everywhere and all the time, especially in our artistic, creative endeavors, that it can start to become detrimental to the creative process. INFJ and INFP people tend to be highly creative and, maybe not so coincidentally, we also come equipped with the intuitive temperament to deal with a high level of instability, especially when it's in the good cause of creating something beautiful.

But that doesn't mean that most other people can understand this.

Added to that is the fact that INFJs and INFPs naturally take the emotional temperature of others and can easily comprehend the subtle energy patterns at play in any group, so we tend to be very aware of how extremely different our thoughts and feelings are, compared to everyone else's. In short, we know we're weird. We also know that much of our behavior, especially when experiencing a creative peak, can look totally crazy to other people.

That's when we go into self-judgement about the instability we experience during periods of high creativity.

The key to overcoming this is self-knowledge. Once we have greater awareness of how we work when we're experiencing a surge in creativity, and awareness of the relationship between the energy of instability and the energy of creativity, we can let go of a lot of the shame we hold around being different. Creative instability might not be something that society at large is comfortable with, but that doesn't mean that it's dangerous or we're going to end up institutionalized if we can't force ourselves to be "normal" like everyone else.

If we accept that this is just the way we are as INFJs and INFPs—people who are born with naturally high levels of creativity and who *need* to express those high levels of creativity, whether that comes out as messy or nonsensical or whatever—the more the mood swings and the mind-all-over-the-place feelings will settle down. Of course, if you feel like your mood swings and extreme feelings are dangerous to you or others, or you suspect you might be struggling with an actual mental illness, then it's best to consult a professional. But if you're like me, and you have the intuition deep down that the instability that's plaguing you is a natural part of your inherent creativity, then it's time to stop pushing it away. The more you let yourself play, the more the energy of instability will feel okay to you.

So, if you have the urge to listen to the same song 76 times in a row, or you feel like you have to pace around and snap your fingers as you talk to imaginary characters out loud, then DO IT. Stop holding back just because it might look crazy from the outside. From this day forward, you know the truth. You *are* mentally unstable, at times, and that's okay. You are just an INFJ or INFP, bursting with creativity.

CHAPTER 3

INFJ Wisdom: Following the White Rabbit

It was Friday night and my husband and I were having pizza with our son while watching a movie. Friday night was always "movie night" in our house, and since our son was only four years old, the movie picks tended to run toward the playful—if not animated—side. This week my son had picked Alice in Wonderland and insisted he didn't want to see the Disney cartoon version, but instead the one with Johnny Depp and Anne Hathaway, so that's what we were watching.

I surprised myself, though, by getting emotional almost immediately after the movie started. Alice had just been proposed to (by a drippy guy she did *not* like) in front of all her friends and family and had gone running off to chase after a white rabbit. There was an extended scene of her running through the twists and turns of the garden, seeing the flash of the white rabbit ahead but not being able to quite keep up with it. Dramatic music played in the background as Alice grew more eager and more desperate to catch the rabbit, more *curious* about where the rabbit came from, why he was dressed in a waistcoat, and where he was heading now.

As I watched this scene something caught in my throat and tears came to my eyes, and as the scene progressed I started to cry even harder. Finally, embarrassed, I got up and discreetly went to the bathroom and closed the door to just let myself have a good old-fashioned cry, the whole time asking myself what could possibly be wrong, but also, at the same time, knowing very well what had triggered me.

I was crying because, for my whole life, to one degree or another, I had been Alice. I was *still* Alice, even though I was almost 40 years old. I had seen my first white rabbit when I was very small, and I had seen too many of them to count since then. Sometimes I went running after them and sometimes I held myself back, but I always, always *saw* them.

I always knew they were there, and that every single one of them contained an invitation all its own.

Like Alice, I had always been *curious*. And that big fat streak of curious in me seemed to be something inborn, something I never could shake, no matter how hard I tried.

Similar to Alice, too, I had been made aware from that same young age that most other people did not see the white rabbits. Or, if they did see them, they immediately dismissed them as pests to keep out of their garden, or trivial little animals not worth paying attention to, or worse, as nothing at all. For most of my life, it seemed that not only was I one of the rare people who saw the white rabbit, but even rarer, I saw that it was wearing a waistcoat and a pocket watch and I wanted to know more. I wanted to know so badly that I got myself into trouble more times than I could count by chasing after it.

This is the INFJ and this is the INFP. We are the people who see the white rabbit. We are also the people who risk many things to go chasing after it.

It's no surprise that *Alice in Wonderland* has remained such a popular classic through the years, because anyone who has read it a few times can see how, like all powerful stories, what appears to be a simple children's tale on the surface actually functions as a container for much larger ideas. Alice is a person who dares to think outside the box and step outside the mainstream. Her journey through Wonderland is a journey of the human mind breaking through limiting belief systems. It's The Matrix before The Matrix was a thing.

That was why I had such a strong reaction to seeing Alice chase that white rabbit. Because I had spent my entire life observing, exploring, and finally, trying to break through as many limiting belief systems in my own mind as I possibly could. For me, there was no other way to live, at least no other way in which I had a decent chance at happiness. If I turned away from the white rabbit, if I shrank away from the invitation to journey through Wonderland out of fear of what I might find there, how my life might change, or worse, what other people might think of me, then I intuitively knew that I would end up miserable and depressed, mired in despair.

For me, Wonderland was the only way. There was never any question of whether I would follow the white rabbit.

The other part of the movie that deeply resonated with me was Johnny Depp in the role of the Mad Hatter. Although the tea party scene is only one relatively short episode in the book and the Disney classic, every oddball eccentric out there knows the tea party scene is where it's at. For us, that scene feels like the epicenter of the whole story, and it is that scene that has spoken to generations of weirdos the world over. Whenever I'm online and see a social media profile that quotes from the tea party scene it's like a bright little sparkly flag that says, "Hey! Over here! I'm weird too!" and I know there's a good chance I and this new person could be friends.

Johnny Depp's version of the Mad Hatter felt so right to me because, as he says, he's "half-mad." For most of my life I have felt "half-mad." I have always been an odd mixture of intelligent and intellectual, but also irrational and, at times, a little insane. I have worried myself sick that maybe I was actually fully insane and just didn't know it. But this never came to pass, and as I got older, I began to realize that I didn't have to be afraid of the way my mind worked. I started to see that, like the Mad Hatter, it was only that I was "half-mad."

I believe that all INFJ and INFP people are "half-mad" in this same way, and by that, I mean our temperament is a mixture of the rational and the irrational, a balance between concrete objectivism and surreal vision. But because we live in a society that is so heavily weighted on the rational side the collective does not value that mixture, or that balance. Society focuses instead almost solely on attributes of the masculine—rationality, logic, action, organization, planning, results and outcome—and ignores most of the attributes of the feminine—

irrationality, feeling, dreaming, nurturing, receiving and patience. There is nothing wrong with the masculine, but when the masculine attributes are the *only* items given validation we fall out of balance. Because life is made up of two sides. The masculine and the feminine. The rational *and* the irrational.

Think about this: The stock market has been studied backward and forward by experts and geniuses and fail-safe computer programs, and all those brains decided that certain things shouldn't happen and probably wouldn't happen, ever. Things like the stock market crash on Black Monday, October 19, 1987. All the mathematical calculations in the world said that a crash like that was so unlikely it was pretty much impossible. *It never should have happened.* But it did. It happened, rationality be damned.

And what about this: During the Vietnam War the US Government fed all the available data it had on the war effort into the most advanced computer they had in those days. They included number of men fighting, number and type of weapons, technical capability of every bit of technology they had, dollars spent, and everything they knew about the other side. They fed all this information into the computer in 1970, when the whole country was in despair over how many lives had been lost and if the horror would ever end, and they asked the computer to tell them when they would win the war and the computer spit out an answer 20 minutes later. *The US won the war in 1965.*

According to pure logic, the war should have been over. But it wasn't. It was five years past the computer's prediction, with no end in sight.

In both cases, people were taken by surprise. The stock market geniuses were knocked so far off-kilter by Black Monday that it took some of them months, even years, to fully emotionally recover and trust the market again. Similarly, after the Vietnam War, nothing was ever the same for the US Government. They, too, had lost trust in their own experts.

But somehow, I think if the Mad Hatter had been present for either of those situations, he wouldn't have been surprised at all. He never would have been thrown out of balance, because his balance was questionable to begin with.

This is the secret to the INFJ's eerie ability to forecast the future, and the INFP's equally unnerving gift of seeing directly into the human heart and accepting whatever is found there, no matter how dark. *We are wise enough to value the irrational.* We are born with a temperament that mixes a discerning intelligence with the truth of being, also, "half-mad." We believe in numbers, in hard data and logic, and amounts measured and weighed—*but only up to a certain point.* And after that point we know, deep in our bones, that really anything could happen. The market could crash out of nowhere. The war could drag on forever, demanding ever more blood and money as payment for the ignorance of men.

How do we know these things? How are we able to work with the irrational in a way that most other people never can?

It's because we live through stories. *Life* is a story. And the INFJs and INFPs of the world know that every story has to come with a fair dose of the irrational, because the irrational is what makes things happen.

The irrational is the event that nudges the main character onto his hero's journey. The irrational is the urge that pushes the villain to commit actions from which she can never turn back. The irrational has its roots—long, twisting, crazy deformed roots—in emotion, in pain, and in the deep, deep darkness of time and the world beneath the world and the human heart.

The irrational is born out of the feminine. It is rich and alive, and constantly fertile.

INFJs and INFPs are born with this energy already a part of us. We are half of this world and half of the other—"half-mad" like the Mad

Hatter—and able to see and accept things that are rejected by mainstream society. This is one of our sources of power, and one of our many gifts. But, we are also like Alice, stuck in a world that either doesn't see or doesn't care about white rabbits, and much of the time we feel like we're left to chase them all on our own.

But as more and more INFJs and INFPs come together and meet each other, form discussion groups, and have conversations online, across time zones and all over the planet, we are beginning to see that we are not the only ones. Some of us are Alice and some of us are the Mad Hatter and most of us fluidly move between one and the other as we see fit, but all of us are, at heart, the same.

All of us are beginning to see that in this crazy new world we're entering, maybe it's okay to be "half-mad."

CHAPTER 4

INFJ Introverted Feeling: Reclaiming Power from Our Raging Inner Child

I originally moved to San Francisco in 2004. I'd lived in Seattle for four years prior to that and basically spent those four years immersed in the bar and club scene and completely wasted. I was a bad alcoholic getting worse and the only possible solution I could think of was to put about a thousand miles between myself and the poisonous environment Seattle had become for me.

Well, when I got to San Francisco, I got sober, but then I fell into a couple of crazy jobs: one at a private detective agency and the next at a startup where the CEO turned out to be an extreme narcissist. I spent the next four years in San Francisco, until 2008, consumed by working long hours and meeting the demands of my boss. Finally, I hit my breaking point. I had to get out.

In the fall of 2008, my husband (then boyfriend) and I landed back in Seattle for the last time. I got yet another crazy job at yet another crazy startup and went directly back into workaholism. I'd managed to stay off the alcohol since 2005, but all my other toxic behaviors were firmly in place. I neglected self-care, routinely skipped meals and sleep, smoked massive amounts of marijuana, and felt like I was on a never-ending hamster wheel of work, all in a desperate attempt to cope with the things in my life that I didn't want to address.

This time, it wasn't long before I hit that breaking point that I knew oh so well. By the summer of 2009 I was burnt out, completely. I was toast. So, I fell back on my old tried-and-true strategy. My husband and I decided to move again. This time back to San Francisco.

I knew it wasn't healthy. I was well aware that I was bouncing around like a ping-pong ball between cities. But, I couldn't see the pattern either. I couldn't make sense of my motivations. In fact, it took me years to piece it all together, and I had to write three autobiographical novels to do it. I wrote *Between the Shadow and Lo*, the first book, to chronicle my journey through alcoholic darkness in Seattle between the years 2000 to 2004, and then followed it up with *West Is San Francisco*, a deep dive into my empath/narcissist relationship with my sociopathic boss at the San Francisco startup. I finished the trilogy off with *Enormous Forces*, a book that narrates my last year back in Seattle from 2008 to 2009.

As weird as this sounds, it was only by writing three long novels that I was able to figure out the pattern. It was only by exploring every theme, every archetype, and every symbol of my experience—and by turning all the people in my real life into fictional characters—that I was able to make sense of anything that had gone down during that intense decade of my life.

By the time I began to understand why I had burned so many bridges over and over again during the years spanning 2000 to 2009, it was 2013. All those events were long in the past. Part of me wished I could have figured it out sooner, but another part of me knew it wasn't destined to happen like that. Beyond those feelings, I knew I needed to dig deeper. I still had to answer my most intriguing question: Why did I always destroy something big in my life, in order to create something new?

It wasn't until I began heavily researching my INFJ personality type that the answer to that question finally began to emerge.

As an INFJ, extraverted feeling is our auxiliary function, which means it comes second in our functional stack. Extraverted feeling is focused on the feelings of *others*, and it is an expert at reading facial expressions, body language, tone of voice, and choice of words. It then takes all that information, integrates it into a workable emotional theory of what's going on with the person, and applies it to real-time situations in order to better negotiate relationships. This is why INFJs are so incredibly skillful at counseling others. We can immediately discern emotional currents in other people and use that discernment to help them discover for themselves what they need.

However, the flip side of this (and also the dark side of it for INFJs, if you ask me) is that because extraverted feeling is found within our primary function stack, the other side of the coin, introverted feeling, falls within our shadow functions. These are the four functions that are driven largely by our unconscious.

Everyone has shadow functions, that's the way personality typing works. We all have four functions that are driven by our conscious mind, and then four more that are driven by the unconscious. We all have darkness within us, that's just part of being human, and we can't fully control it. However, it is helpful for INFJs to be aware of our shadow functions and how they operate if they're not acknowledged, especially when an INFJ is stressed out, which is the most likely time that our shadow functions will show up and come into play.

Introverted feeling, as mentioned above, is a cognitive function found on the INFJ's shadow side. It is the function that deals with a person's own individual feelings and beliefs. *Not the feelings of others.* This is so important for INFJs to understand because there is a tendency for INFJs to assume that because we are so adept with other people's emotions we also probably have a halfway decent understanding of our own. Well, yes and no. A healthy, non-stressed-at-the-moment INFJ who is mature and grounded definitely has the ability to sit with their feelings and parse them out. But, I would argue, a stressed-out INFJ who overall feels desperately unfulfilled and dissatisfied in life actually cannot rely on this skill nearly as much.

When you have an INFJ who is deeply unhappy, feels unheard and unseen, and/or is struggling with big life issues, and has no effective tools to deal with the situation, you end up with an INFJ who is carrying a festering sore of introverted feeling deep inside and that sore is just getting bigger and uglier and more painful by the minute. And because we're so stressed out, we can't even see the sore for what it is.

We just know we're in pain and we want it to stop. In the case of a personality with introverted feeling as part of the primary function stack, in times of great stress, pain like this might serve as an emotional compass that guides the individual towards what needs to be adjusted or how things could be improved, nudging them to an upgrade in their life.

But because introverted feeling falls on the shadow side for INFJs, when we're stressed out, it doesn't work like that at all for us.

Because INFJs can't figure out our own emotions when we're under a lot of stress, it's easy to fall even deeper into our shadow. It's also important to remember that, psychologically speaking, the shadow contains all that is most primitive in us, all that is child-like and undeveloped. So, basically, the deeper you go into your shadow, the more immature and childish the version you will find of yourself there. This is not a bad thing, it's just an inner child thing. Our shadow encompasses all the parts of ourselves we are afraid to own, everything that we are embarrassed or ashamed of in some way. That includes the little boy or little girl in each of us that is terrified and full of pain and rage.

When an INFJ becomes extremely stressed out and is deeply unhappy with their life situation and is also blocked from figuring out their own emotions about why they are so unhappy and what needs to change, they become more frustrated by the day. Their introverted feeling continues to fester until it's ready to blow, and that introverted feeling only has the tools and mindset of a four-year-old child. This is when we find INFJs making the worst choices. This is when we see INFJs becoming intensely determined to carry out actions based on the most absurd logic. Because in this state, the only solution that appears rational to an INFJ is the one that is the most extreme: Burn everything down. Start over.

That's what I was doing when I bounced from Seattle to San Francisco and then back again. I was so stressed out, so caught in addiction and constant drama, that my introverted feeling had reached a crisis point. When it exploded, I felt my only option was to burn my bridges and abandon my existing situation for something out of left field, something totally new.

Now, sometimes it's actually a great thing to burn your life down and start over. Taking that sort of action is part of the journey for some people. However, in the case of most stressed-out INFJs, there is no need to burn everything down. The structure itself, the architecture of the INFJ's life, is really not all that bad. There are some big flaws, sure, but what it honestly needs is a couple of significant shifts and then a lot of little tweaks. It needs patience and a realistic view of how long things might take before improvement is seen, and an acceptance of how setbacks are a normal part of the process.

However, the festering, raging, extremely pissed-off four-year-old introverted feeling of the INFJ is totally incapable of patience and acceptance and getting real about the situation.

This is an issue that crops up time and again for most of us INFJs, much to our chagrin. Rest assured, it keeps showing up because it's something we badly need to work on. It's one of our Achilles' heels that always seems to bring us down, and if we can approach it with better tools, we won't be taken down by it so often.

One of the strategies we can use to avoid this pitfall is to start writing, or to engage more deeply with our writing if we're already in a practice with it. By writing our life events as memoir or turning them into autobiographical fiction, or even just making it a habit to journal our thoughts on a regular basis, we're able to get distance between ourselves and our emotions. We can then view our feelings from the outside, just as we would when counseling someone else. This is the method that worked so well for me after I came out of the whirlwind of addiction, dysfunction, and sudden moves that plagued me for almost ten years. By turning the events of my life into a story I was able to zoom out and get the big picture view. I could then see the pattern that had eluded me and take steps to remedy things by doing exactly what I would have recommended for another.

Transforming our lives into story works wonderfully in the aftermath. However, sometimes the aftermath is too late. For INFJs who are in the grip of destructive introverted feeling and need help right now, the best way to get around this weakness, and maybe even turn it into a strength, is to learn how to ask for help from other people.

INFJs who are considering burning their lives down and who remain isolated and alone in the situation will go deeper and deeper into their heads. We will totally immerse ourselves in fantasy-land thinking about how great it's going to be on the other side, after we've burned the bridge that's giving us so much trouble. We will feed this fantasy with obsessive thinking to the point that it overrides our natural intuition and seems real to us, and like there could be no other outcome. We will steadfastly ignore the fact that our intuition has always told us before that every situation has many possible outcomes because we will be so driven and focused on making *this one thing* happen in *exactly this way* and then, at some point, our house of cards will collapse, and we will be left devastated, confused, and floating sadly among the debris of the relationship, career, or life situation that we just torched with glee a few days, or hours, before.

But, if the INFJ brings other people into the situation—our spouse, our best friend, or someone else we trust—in order to seek outside feedback, we stand a much better chance of finding a way to make the shift we need to make, without destroying the good parts of our life in the process. If the INFJ is committed to staying open to feedback from other types—thinkers and perceivers and sensors—and communicating our feelings and needs honestly, we will begin to see how we can improve the existing structures of our lives without completely trashing them and starting over.

This is hard, because INFJs have a tendency toward arrogance. Our introverted intuition is usually so accurate that it's easy to fall into the trap of assuming we don't need anyone else's opinion when it comes time for us to make a decision. But part of growing into ourselves as INFJs is accepting that others are strong in areas where we may be weak. It's being humble enough to ask for help when we need it, and also realizing there may solutions available that we're unable to see before someone else points them out to us.

As counterintuitive as it may sound to us, sometimes the person an INFJ needs most is that realistic, thinking, sensor-type of individual who can pull us back down to earth. If we can accept the gifts of other personality types—gifts that are so much different than ours—we will be much better off.

And we won't end up spontaneously throwing so much of the good in our life into a bonfire.

CHAPTER 5

INFJs and Multi-Layered Reality: Welcoming the Complexity of Our Relationships

When I was a teenager I had a boyfriend who couldn't stay out of trouble. We got together when I was 15 and he was 16, and we stayed together for the next four years—with a lot of ups and downs in between. To say we had a rocky relationship doesn't even begin to describe our dynamic. We fought constantly, and it was always the screaming-and-throwing-dishes-at-each-other kind of fights. He cheated on me (a lot), I cheated on him (a little), and we manipulated and betrayed each other at every turn.

About a year and a half into the relationship things started getting violent. He gave me two black eyes on two separate occasions and, more than once, I hit him with a belt. I believe that to this day his bicep still retains the perfect imprint of my teeth, upper and lower rows, from one particular incident when he tried to throw me out of his house by dumping me over the railing of his porch and I latched on like a Jack Russell Terrier and refused to let go. He also stole my car, and my checkbook, because, in addition to being sexually compulsive, he was also somewhat of a kleptomaniac.

When I was going through all this stuff with this horrible relationship, a lot of other people threw a lot of judgment at me. Family members, friends, coworkers, teachers, and other random people I went to school with. The consensus was strong regarding a couple of basic concepts, and I was routinely urged to buy into these concepts: I was good. He was bad. I was a bright young woman from a good home with a promising future. He was a thug who was going nowhere. I was the victim. He was the perpetrator.

Only, it didn't *feel* that way, to me. Not at all.

Yes, my family had money and worked white-collar jobs and everyone in it went to college and knew how to navigate the social and economic waters of America quite well. And yes, my boyfriend's mother had had three children by the time she was 18 and some of those kids ended up in foster care and he had grown up in poverty and most of the men in his family ended up in jail.

But that didn't mean we didn't have a whole lot of other things in common.

My father was an alcoholic, and so was my boyfriend's father. My mother had died when I was young, and I'd never fully recovered from the trauma of it. My boyfriend's mother had told him she'd never wanted him to begin with, and he'd never recovered from the trauma of that either. By the time I hit 15 I was grappling with enormous amounts of grief and pain and rage that I couldn't express and—as a bright young woman from a good home—was encouraged to ignore. It was immensely satisfying to find someone who felt that same grief and pain and rage, but instead of suppressing it, chose instead to act out, steal, lie, fight and hit and punch something, anything, that got in his way.

When I was in that intense relationship with my extremely troubled boyfriend, I never felt like a victim, although I did go through periods where I blamed him for the whole fucked up experience we were having together. But, still, I never felt like I was "good," and he was "bad." I never felt like if he "treated me better," which is what everyone around me said, then everything would be all right. It was so much more complex than that. Both of us were people who were scared and struggling and utterly entangled in toxic thinking and dysfunctional coping methods. What we were doing together, the experience we were having, couldn't be reduced to some sort of simplistic formula wherein a good boyfriend does certain things for his good girlfriend and if either one strays outside of what's expected then someone has done wrong and gets labeled as the villain. My boyfriend wasn't a villain and he didn't need to be punished. Living inside of the life he was creating for himself was already punishment enough.

Oddly enough, the hardest part of this whole situation, for me, was the strong underlying current of self-doubt I constantly felt about it. All the people in my life at that time saw my situation from one particular point of view, and that point of view was very black-and-white, very easy to grasp. It also made rational sense. I mean, it's not like I was in the dark about why all these people hated my boyfriend and felt the way they did. I got it. But that didn't change the fact that I couldn't alter the way *I* saw it and the way *I* was experiencing things.

In my view, my boyfriend was a complicated individual. He committed himself to choices and actions that hurt people and damaged himself. He was impulsive, aggressive, and destructive. But he was also kind and good with people. He was funny and smart and creative. On top of all that he was constantly anxious—and occasionally terrified—that he was worthless and unlovable. He had been hit many times in his life, as well as lied to and betrayed. As he grew into a man, he ended up doing all of these things to others.

He was a bundle of good and bad, light and dark, it was just that most of his darkness had been externalized, and so most other people could easily see it.

This was where I kept coming up short in my quest to find compassionate non-judgment from others. Was that relationship toxic? Yes. Was it dangerous to my health? Yes, on so many levels. But was it devoid of meaning? No. Was my boyfriend a person who should have been villainized? Again, no.

As a young INFJ, my brain had an extremely difficult time making sense of these questions and I got no firm answers. It wasn't until years later, when I discovered my INFJ-ness, and began meeting other intuitives and learning from them, that I understood much more clearly what had been going on.

For an INFJ, nothing falls into a black-or-white category, especially not people or relationships.

From a very young age, I have experienced reality as multi-layered. I see the first layer as the physical reality that surrounds us, the data that can be taken in through our five senses, and concretely proved or disproved through the scientific method. I see the second layer as a more personal emotional reality—the intangible thoughts and feelings and desires and repulsions experienced within my own self, and the selves of others, which isn't visible on the surface. Now that I'm older I also see the third layer, an energetic reality which contains the interconnectedness of all beings. In my view, all three realities are intertwined. For every ripple, another ripple is created and spreads outward, without end.

Because of the way I view reality, because of the way I *experience* it, relationships come packaged with a different meaning for me. I am not interested in only interacting with people whom I deem "pleasant" or whom I can easily understand. I also need something more than only having external characteristics in common with someone, like being the same age or them also having children, in order for me to consider a relationship worthwhile. Because I experience reality as multi-layered, and because one of my core beliefs is that I am here to learn and grow as a soul, the primary element that must be present for me to initiate a relationship with someone is that I find them *compelling*.

To me, "compelling" roughly translates into the feeling that a certain person has something for me, some piece of knowledge that I need to complete part of the big picture within my own mind. It's an intuitive hunch that the person is expressing a certain energetic pattern that I would like to learn more about. Some might call this a karmic relationship. As in, I've had past lives with that person and so, in this life, we're supposed to come together again to work something out. Honestly, I'm not always sure why I find some people so compelling and others leave me cold. What I do know is that I can't cursorily label people as “nice” or “asshole.” I can’t put people in little boxes and then judge the boxes I don’t like as wrong or bad.

This is not to say that I haven’t experienced my fair share of toxic people who I ultimately had to cut out of my life, my old boyfriend being one of them. We all experience those kinds of people and relationships at some point, no matter what our personality type is. But INFJs and INFPs handle it differently from most other types. No matter how frequently or badly we get burned by others, it seems we simply cannot help but see that every person is a complex being. We are incapable of writing people off, without thinking more deeply about it first.

As a teenager, I never thought of this willingness to see the complexity in every human being as a skill. In fact, I didn’t even have the tools or language at that time to explain or understand what I was doing. My need to consider people and situations from all sides—examining every facet without judgment—before I could make a decision, seemed to be something that only set me apart. I was frequently told that I was gullible or naïve. It was implied that I was weak in some way for giving people so many chances. For years I tried to toughen up and be more unforgiving. I tried to label certain people as stupid, or even evil. But it never worked. It didn’t make me feel any better to shut down my compassion, it only made me feel worse.

In today’s world, we are increasingly at risk of falling prey to a collective mindset that judges, condemns, and punishes people based on scant information and polarized opinion. It’s now routine to see someone’s flaws and faults exposed on the internet, quickly followed by a mob of people who are so ugly and brutal in their comments toward that person that it’s truly staggering. We are able to villainize, outcast, and shun individuals on a scale never before seen.

This is why we need the compassionate wisdom of intuitive people like we never have before in the history of civilization. Our technological skills are developing so rapidly that everyone is having a hard time keeping up, but in the emotional realm we continue to remain primitive, lost, and sometimes even savage. INFJs and INFPs have the ability to be a voice of reason that can counteract the brutality and ugliness of the mob mentality, rebalancing humanity back toward the sane and loving end of the spectrum.

We have to recognize the value of our skills, though, and realize that we are born with the ability to see past the surface of a person for a reason. It's time to realistically assess ourselves and understand that we are not gullible, naïve, or weak, and that, instead, we have the potential to be empowered around our gift of true sight into a person's soul.

Along with these realizations comes responsibility. As energetically sensitive beings, INFJs and INFPs must step up and claim ownership around our boundaries and our unique point of view. It's inevitable that other people will lash out with projections and negative judgments when we express our compassionate, and sometimes unpopular, opinions in any sort of public forum. If we have done our homework, we'll know how to handle that sort of energy and move through it unscathed.

Choosing to see my old boyfriend as a multi-layered human being, as well as an individual worthy of forgiveness, was not easy. Choosing to see our relationship as a vehicle that served both of us in the purpose of learning wasn't easy either. But it helped me grow as a person by leaps and bounds. Every single one of our relationships, no matter how difficult they are at the time, has the power to do this. But it's up to us to choose forgiveness, compassion, and the vision needed to access that power.

It's up to us to embrace our gift of true sight into someone else's soul, our ability to see the bundle of good and bad, light and dark, all mixed together in one complex web of energy.

CHAPTER 6
INFJs and the Biofield: We Are Intuitive Healers AND Wireless Receivers

In March of 2017 I was sitting in a hospital room in Ann Arbor, Michigan watching my dad as he passed in and out of unconsciousness. He'd been diagnosed with a brain tumor the year before and his decline had been rapid and brutal. He'd been a workaholic surgeon in New York City and had gone, literally, from performing surgery one day to being hospitalized himself the next. It was now 11 months after his initial diagnosis and I'd flown in from California the night before when he was admitted back into the hospital. He was in septic shock and it wasn't clear how long he had left.

My brother had dropped me off at the hospital earlier and then gone to get something to eat. He'd been living with my dad for the past year and been his primary caretaker, so I knew he needed the break. Now, it was only me and a friend of one of my uncles, a guy named Tom, who sat watching my dad toss and turn as we made small talk with the nurses who came in and out of the room to check his vital signs. As we sat and waited, for what we didn't yet know, we also talked between ourselves.

"You know, I remember the funniest story about your grandfather," Tom said. "I'm not sure why it's coming to me now, but it's something I'll never forget."

With that, Tom began to tell me his funny story that really wasn't funny at all. When he said "funny" he didn't mean humorous, but funny in the way that odd and strange things are, things for which you have no explanation and so, as Stephen King says, you just kind of pop them into an open file in your mind and only think about them from time to time, never quite coming to a conclusion about what they mean.

It was the middle of the 1970s, maybe 1975 or 1976, Tom thought, and he had been with my grandfather and my uncle in New York City. My grandfather had also been a surgeon, like my father, although at that time my dad was still finishing up his residency in Detroit. Tom and my uncle and my grandfather had been walking down an extremely crowded sidewalk at a fast clip. Tom said people were streaming by them, so fast they seemed to go by in a blur. But then suddenly my grandfather stopped. He froze in his tracks and then turned to look at a woman who had just passed. "One minute," he said to Tom and my uncle, and then he walked quickly toward the woman to catch up with her.

"Well, we didn't know what was going on," Tom told me. My grandfather and this woman sat down on a stoop, on the steps of an apartment building. "They talked intensely for about 15 minutes," Tom said. "Then they both got up again and she shook his hand and was just beaming, and then she went on her way."

My mind tried to put together the pieces of the puzzle, but I was stumped.

"So…I guess I don't get it?" I finally said.

Tom chuckled, but again, not in the way you laugh at something funny, but in that way that sometimes you laugh because you don't know what else to do. It's the only reaction to have because you have no way of making sense of what happened.

"Your grandfather came back to us," he said. "And he told us, 'That woman has cancer and is on chemotherapy. She's very ill but I knew I could tell her some things that might make the chemo go a little better for her.'"

They were stunned, Tom said. How could he possibly have known she had cancer? Or was on chemotherapy? She had looked completely normal to everyone else.

"I saw her face," my grandfather told them. "I saw her face, and I just knew." And that was all he said.

As Tom told me this story I got chills, but I couldn't express what was going on in my heart and my mind. I came from a line of doctors, a lineage of healers, but my family was also eminently pragmatic. They were all very mental in their approach to the world. Very logical and rational. My "hippie New Age" outlook had never gone over well with them, if they even stopped long enough to pay attention to anything I actually said.

How did my grandfather know that woman was ill when she looked perfectly ordinary to everyone else? How had he been able to pinpoint, not only that she was sick, but her type of sickness, the treatment she was going through, and the fact that it was the treatment that was now making her suffer so much, not the illness? How had he been able to discern all of this in the half second it took for her to pass him on a crowded street and, also in that half second, been able to make the snap decision to go after her and access the information she needed to help her heal?

Well, as my grandfather said at the time, he "saw her face" and he "just knew."

I suspect that if anyone had questioned my grandfather more deeply on any of this at the time, he would have grown uncomfortable and shrugged the whole thing off. He definitely would not have believed that maybe there was something about *him*, something he carried inherently in his makeup, that allowed him to recognize illness from the inside rather than from the outside, in the people around him.

I don't know the personality types of my grandfather or my father, and as both are now deceased, I'll probably never know. But I'm willing to bet that even if they weren't INFJ or INFP types, they were some sort of NF (intuitive feeler) or NT (intuitive thinker) type. I think it was my grandfather's intuition that let him access the information he needed from that woman, in the less than one second that it took her to pass him on the street. And I don't think that this "intuition" of his was something nebulous, magical, or possibly imaginary.

On the contrary, I believe the intuition of the NF and NT types is something very real.

In the past couple of decades, scientists have begun researching something called the "biofield." It depends on who you ask for the definition, but basically, the biofield is defined as the energetic matrix that surrounds the physical body. It is scientifically recognized that the human body generates multiple electromagnetic fields, with the heart generating one of the largest. The biofield is, in the scientific view, another one of these electromagnetic fields. In my view, which would be categorized as the "New Age" view, the biofield carries much more than an electrical charge.

I believe the biofield surrounding each person contains every detail of the energy signature of that person. Traumas, memories, desires, impulses, illness, vitality, and so much more. I also believe that intuitive people, most especially INFJs and INFPs, are born with an exceptional ability to access the biofields of others, instantly, and also if need be, across time and space. I believe that *every* human can function "wirelessly," but that INFJs and INFPs in particular seem to be born with incredible wireless capacities, an extraordinary ability to "receive" from others.

This is what I think happened with my grandfather and that woman, who was no more than a stranger to him, so long ago. Because her biofield carried such a strong energy of illness it broadcasted itself to him loud and clear when he passed her on the street. He didn't need time to make a diagnosis. He received her biofield feedback the same way the human ear hears a train whistle. We don't need a few minutes or even a few seconds to receive the soundwaves into our ears and make sense of what that sound is. If it's a familiar sound, then we know it *the instant it happens*. Same thing with sight. We don't look at an apple and need a few minutes to figure out what it is. If we've seen an apple before then we know, *that very second.* My grandfather had already been a doctor for many years before he passed that woman on the street. His intuitive ability already knew cancer, and so when he passed that woman he only needed to take one look at her face in order to access the information in her biofield.

I believe this is also why INFJs and INFPs are so attracted to wounded people. I've had many instances in my life where I was strongly compelled to talk to someone, get to know someone better, or bring someone into my life, only to find out later that they were suffering from great unresolved trauma which I seemed to be especially equipped to help with due to one "coincidental" reason or another. It's not everyone with a wound, of course, because almost the entire population has wounds of one sort or another, but it *is* people who are in active psychic pain that matches my specific healing abilities. Those people attract me like no one else, even if I try to fight it.

I think INFJs and INFPs are born with this ability to wirelessly receive and access the biofield of other humans so effortlessly because we are meant to help. We are born healers. Just as certain breeds of dog have an inborn temperament to be helpers to humanity and thrive when they work as guide dogs or herders or guards, INFJs and INFPs are a certain breed of people who also have an inborn temperament that thrives when it can be of help in healing someone else.

That's what it feels like, too, for me. It feels like I'm a dog sniffing something out when I'm talking to someone or observing someone, and I realize they have a wound inside them, a wound they're actively working on and need assistance to heal. I'll be having a conversation and everything is normal and then suddenly it hits me like a lightning bolt. I just suddenly *know* that there is something about this person I want to pay closer attention to and figure out. Once the energy Bloodhound in me sniffs around long enough and I can be sure of what I'm feeling, sure of the confirmation of my diagnosis, then I feel this little laser focus thing inside of me activate and start gearing up to help.

Even if science doesn't yet have the information or the terminology to address this puzzling ability of the INFJ and the INFP, that doesn't mean it isn't real. Or that we're exaggerating or making things up. The intuitive "hits" we get about people are valid, and our unrelenting urge to help heal others is valid too. For too long, we've been made to believe that our abilities are nonsense and the way we get entangled with others is all our fault, that we're codependent, have poor boundaries, need too much approval, or can't stand up for ourselves. That we are weak in some way, and flawed.

Nothing could be further from the truth. We are not weak, or flawed. We have extraordinary abilities and in the next century the science will emerge to show the truth of that.

In the meantime, we'll carry on as we always have. Helping wherever we can.

CHAPTER 7

INFJs as Empowered Healers: Moving Beyond the Fixing and Saving Dynamic

In 2009 I was living back in Seattle, after a crazy four years in San Francisco, and working at my second startup. It was the most drama-filled job I'd had yet, and that was really saying something. Our tiny organization limped along from month to month, always on the verge of running out of money and on the brink of crisis. I had started as the secretary but quickly moved into taking on various roles, working tech support when needed and spending most of my time assisting the CEO as he waded through every new hot mess that unfolded seemingly every week.

I had also quickly become friends with one of the only other women on staff, the executive who ran our product management team and lived in San Diego, and who flew up to Seattle for two or three days each week to work in the office with us. I had been immediately attracted to her from the first moment we met. She was smart as hell and an incredibly original thinker. She had multiple degrees in engineering and she looked like a supermodel. For some reason, she seemed to want to be friends with me too, and we established a routine of going out together after work on the days she was in town.

As I got to know this woman, I discovered that her perfect genius bombshell exterior was just an expertly crafted mask. Inside, she was a mess. Her marriage was falling apart, and she had never wanted the kids she now had with her husband. She had a long history of abuse, molestation, and other assorted traumas beginning in childhood and holding strong right up into adulthood. I also noticed that she had problems with substance abuse, lying, and sexual compulsion.

All in all, she was a basket case.

As the months wore on, this woman's self-destructive behavior began to affect everyone in the office. No one knew when she was telling the truth and when she was hiding important information. She got extremely drunk on occasions when we needed her to keep a clear head. She began to spend more and more time in Seattle too, in order to get away from the marriage she so desperately wanted to leave behind.

I still kept hanging out with her after work, two or three times a week, every week.

However, the more time I spent with her, the worse I felt. Every evening after seeing her I felt drained, if not utterly exhausted. I wasn't ever sure when she was telling me the truth either, so I always vacillated between getting angry at some injustice that had been done to her by someone else in the office, or suspicious and doubtful about what she was telling me. I noticed that I had started to dread Tuesdays, which was when she flew into town, and look forward to Thursdays, the day she left.

But still, I kept hanging out with her.

Because she had confided in me, and because I knew all about her past, I couldn't let go. Yes, she lied about a lot of stuff, but I could tell the abuse wasn't one of the things she was lying about. It was obvious in the way she used alcohol and became sexually compulsive when drunk. I had seen the pattern before and knew that she honestly was a very damaged person.

As the weeks went by, my husband questioned me about my friendship with this woman. *Why was I sticking around?* he asked. She was obviously a ticking time bomb, just waiting to self-destruct. I didn't try to explain myself, because I knew that any explanation I could give would come out sounding flimsy and lame. And because inside, I knew the truth of why I stayed. *I want to help her*, was what I thought, every time he asked me, even though I never said it.

This has been a recurring pattern my entire life.

When I was in junior high I had a good friend who came from a bad home and was mostly interested in sex and partying. I spent the next two years trying to drag her into good grades and better interests. It didn't work.

When I first moved to Seattle I became friends with a young woman who had so much abuse in her past I couldn't keep track of all the different violations she listed to me. She had a penchant for violent boyfriends and cocaine. I spent the next four years trying to build up her self-esteem. It didn't work.

When I was in my early 20s another one of my friends became addicted to meth and stopped paying his rent. I was convinced that if I paid his rent for a couple months to give him a little financial breathing room he would be able to start getting his life together and get into rehab. It didn't work.

I could list at least a dozen more examples, but I think you get the picture.

I have spent much of my life feeling alternately guilty and flawed for succumbing time and again to the temptation to throw myself into quicksand with the drowning person, and then angry and judgmental against others because they can't see how badly the person needs help.

But as I've gotten to know more INFJs and INFPs, I don't feel nearly as bad about this whole "heal-fix-save" pattern I've had going on with so many people. Because it seems that almost all other INFJs and INFPs have it too.

In fact, I didn't even know there was such a name for this pattern as "heal-fix-save" until I started watching videos done by a guy named Lee Harris, one of my all-time favorite energy intuitives, on Youtube. If you haven't seen his videos yet and you're an INFJ or an INFP, I highly recommend them. Google "Lee Harris energy." Lee and his videos are life changing.

Lee Harris frequently talks about how there are so many intuitive people that have this heal-fix-save thing going on with our energy, and I wholeheartedly agree with him. As previously mentioned when I talked about the biofield, I think there is something in INFJs and INFPs, something that has to do with the way we are wired, that points us toward healing people who are carrying an energetic imbalance. However, what happens a lot of the time, is that we move from the intention of "heal" to the intention of "fix" very quickly, almost before we know what's happened. And if the party in question has severe damage going on, we can then move even further down the spectrum, into "save" territory. Again, it can happen so fast that we're not even consciously aware of it.

In my opinion, this occurs because of two different, yet intertwined, reasons.

Number one: INFJs and INFPs are not sufficiently aware of the way we work, the way our intuitive abilities work, and/or how to balance ourselves and our gifts in a healthy way.

This was my experience for pretty much the first 32 years of my life. I had no idea how intuitive I was. I alternated between thinking I was crazy, or that other people must experience life just like I did but seemed to be able to handle it much better. I absolutely did not realize how vulnerable I was to the energy of others or how much it could influence me.

Number two: The person we are trying to fix and save is carrying issues that are so similar to ours that we are deeply triggered by them and we want to heal that person in order to continue the healing process in ourselves.

This is what happened with me and the executive woman in Seattle. Because she was an alcoholic, and became sexually compulsive when she was drunk, she reminded me so much of my past self that I couldn't see that she had no interest in seeking out healing at that time. She only wanted more self destruction. If my own personal issues hadn't muddied the waters, I would have gained clarity sooner and been able to cut her loose that much faster.

This is why—as with my situation with that woman in Seattle and with INFJ and INFP relationship dynamics overall—the key to understanding the whole heal-fix-save issue, and why it bites us in the ass so much, is to slow down to evaluate the situation clearly, and to make the distinction between healing, and fixing and saving.

Healing work is a process you can *assist* with, and if an outside party assists, it usually will go much faster. Doctors, nurses, therapists (physical and other), acupuncturists, energy workers, or even just a good friend who is willing to listen, all *help* other people along in their healing process. In order to initiate healing, though, the person who needs help needs to be onboard with their own process. It won't work if the person is being dragged kicking and screaming into it.

Fixing and saving is a whole different thing. Fixing is showing up with a toolbox and repairing something *for* someone else. So, I nail your kitchen cabinet back into place as you stand there and watch me because you either can't do it on your own, or you don't want to do it on your own. That works fine if it really is carpentry work that we're talking about. But in the case of healing, doing something *for* someone else because they can't or don't want to do it takes us right back to dragging the kicking and screaming person into the process. It doesn't work.

Saving gets even more extreme. Saving takes the energy of fixing, amps it up, and then throws a good strong dose of self-sacrifice into the mix. There's a reason many Christians describe themselves as "saved," because the self-sacrifice of Jesus is the essential element in the mix.

Now, it doesn't matter if you are totally religious or totally not, no matter who you are, you are definitely not Jesus Christ. And you can nail yourself to a cross for all sorts of people, but every time you do, I guarantee you, that person is not only *not* going to appreciate your attempt to save them, they are going to energetically feel like you're trying to control them, and then they will resist your good intentions even more strongly.

So, if we INFJs and INFPs have this inborn wiring to heal people that can apparently easily go haywire and then we start trying to fix and save everyone who doesn't want it, how do we turn it off? *Can* we turn it off? And is that really the answer? After all, maybe we were born this way for a reason. Maybe our healing abilities were meant to do just that, heal.

The first step is to work with your energy as consciously as possible. That means asking hard questions. Like, does the person you are trying to fix or save actually want to heal at this time? If the answer is no, then do not pass go, do not collect two hundred dollars. If the answer is yes, then comes another hard question. Why are you trying to do the work for them? Why are you attached to their outcome? Can you admit that they might be better served by someone who is able to *assist* them in their healing process from a neutral stance, someone like an objective therapist?

The second step is to continuously do your own inner work by examining your own issues. Are there certain problems that trigger you because you used to suffer from those problems too? Or maybe you've seen your parents or another close loved one struggle with the same issues?

Once you are able to identify and recognize what's going on in your own mind, heart, and soul, it becomes much easier to step back from situations that bring out your fix-and-save compulsions. However, this doesn't mean that your own problem with heal-fix-save will be "fixed" forever. You are an INFJ/INFP personality after all, and you're going to have this tendency all your life. I've found it's most helpful to shift perspective on the issue, and instead of seeing it as a problem, seeing it as something you were born to do. For instance, German Shepherds are born to herd sheep. It's a neutral trait that can be helpful or unhelpful depending on the situation. If there are sheep around, great. We need that German Shepherd to do its thing. If not, the dog might end up trying to herd cats, which never works and only causes chaos.

If there is no one around us interested in healing and needing assistance with the process, INFJs and INFPs are like that German Shepherd with no sheep. We start trying to use our abilities on whoever happens to be in the room with us. The best solution to this is for INFJs and INFPs to be consciously aware of our need to help others with healing, and to put ourselves in situations where people are looking for that exact thing. So, even if you're not ready to make a career change to counselor, maybe you could look into volunteering your time on the weekends to answer the phones for a help line. Or you could help pick up garbage at your local beach, because helping the earth heal counts too.

The more you become conscious of your part in the healing process for others, and how essential it is that you share your gifts with others in that area, the less you will try to rescue the drowning people who don't want to be rescued. The less chance there is, also, that those drowning people will take you down with them.

That's important because, if you are an INFJ and INFP, you are here to heal. Fixing and saving are only detours that take you off your true path.

CHAPTER 8

INFJs in Love: Owning Our Desire for Soul Connection

From the very first moment he walked into my life, I felt it. Although I didn't know what "it" was at the time. It was only later, months later, after we had gotten to know each other, that I looked back on that first meeting and saw exactly how immediate the attraction had been. He had come to our office for a business meeting and I was the one who escorted him to the conference room. On the way there, I felt funny. Tingly. But we had exchanged less than five words. There was no reason for it. So, I shook the feeling off and forgot all about it.

Now, it was eight months later. The guy had joined our staff and so we worked together in the same office. We didn't work in the same area or on the same team, but that hadn't stopped us from getting to know each other. Even though there was no reason for us to conduct more than passingly polite conversation, we'd somehow gotten to talking a number of times, about everything. Psychology, history, life purpose, how the universe works and what's behind it—*everything*.

Now, I was *strongly* attracted. In fact, if I was being honest with myself, I was a little bit in love with the guy. Okay, a lot in love.

However, I was no stranger to INFJ love. The things I experienced when in that state, well, scared me. I got very intense, very fast. I wanted to know every single thing about the person I loved, while hiding most of my own things safely away. I wanted to be as close as possible to the man I was in love with, but then I needed long breaks away where I couldn't talk to him or see him because I was so overwhelmed by the energy surges I experienced around him.

On top of that, I was married. I'd been in a long-term, very happy relationship with my husband, for 15 years.

This was not the first time I'd fallen in love with someone else. By my count, since I'd gotten together with my husband, I tended to fall in love with someone new every three or four years. I had a couple of close friends that I could talk to about these occurrences, but when it came to almost everyone else, it was impossible to explain. The first time it happened I felt HORRIBLE. Even though I didn't act on my feelings at the time, I felt like I was emotionally cheating on my husband. I lived for months in a state of turmoil—bursting with love and desire for someone else, and full of despair about what this might mean for my marriage.

The turning point came when I bit the bullet and finally told my husband how I felt. To my immense relief, he didn't hate me. In fact, he said he'd gone through it too. Because he's an INTJ, he was much more rational about it, but he still *got* it. After that first conversation, we had more long, deep talks and he was the one who helped me see that every relationship is unique. Just because I wanted to explore a romantic connection with someone else, didn't necessarily mean I wanted to break my marriage contract or my romantic connection with him. My husband made it clear to me that he didn't feel any less loved because of my tendency to fall in love with others.

This is a tricky thing for INFJs and INFPs, because I think a lot of us have this tendency toward falling in love more than a few times in our lives. At the core, we are full of love, and we are also driven by people. Deep down, we are hopeless romantics and moonstruck poets, even though we can pull the coldest of poker faces when needed. In my experience, most INFJs and INFPs also crave long-term, serious, committed relationships. We don't like hopping from bed to bed, or heart to heart. When we find someone who is special to us, they are extraordinarily special. But we have huge hearts, and those huge hearts have the capacity to hold more than one special person at a time.

One of my all-time favorite personal growth authors, Steve Pavlina, talks frequently on his blog about a concept he calls "4D connection." He says there are four different types of connections you can have with a person: mental, heart, spiritual, and sexual. If you have a 4D connection with someone, that means you connect with them at every level. It's also possible to enjoy a great relationship with someone if you only have three, or even just two, of the connections with them. This helped me make sense of my own desires as I started to unpack my feelings around my marriage and this other beautiful man who came into my life.

I'm sure there are many people out there who can rationally understand the intensity of attraction one person can experience for another. But, for INFJs and INFPs, this goes so far beyond the rational that we ourselves don't all the time understand what is happening to us when we fall in love. As an INFJ, when I fall, I fall hard. I cannot escape the frantic, intense mixture of desperate joy and pain I experience when in the presence of my beloved. No matter if we're already in a committed relationship or not, INFJs and INFPs can end up feeling nerve-wracked, baffled, and in constant anguish over what seems to other people to be nothing more than a simple crush.

For most of my life I have tried to hide my reaction to falling in love with someone because it makes me feel like a crazy stalker and like something's seriously wrong with me. It's only been in the past few years, since I discovered I'm an INFJ and the unique way that I'm wired, that I've started to understand why I react the way I do, and also accept myself for what I am.

In a word, I'm intense. I sometimes feel emotional energy so strongly—my own and others—that I feel like I'm dizzy. Or like I'm going to vomit or suddenly cry, or both. When I'm around someone with whom I have heavy sexual tension, I feel my own *and I feel theirs*. This makes for a double whammy of intoxicating hormonal sexual juiciness, and sometimes it feels like it's going to blow my circuits. In fact, rarely do I have to actually have sex with the person to feel like I've already been in bed with them.

In addition to this, not only do INFJs and INFPs want authentic, intimate, long-term committed relationships with someone we deeply love and cherish, but we also easily fall in love with people with whom we feel we have an exceptionally strong soul connection. These soul connections are important to INFJs and INFPs because they influence the trajectory of our life. They're not just random physical attractions like so much of the rest of the population seems to experience.

This is why I am attracted to so very few people. Because even though I seem to fall in love with someone new like clockwork, every three or four years, it does take those few years to pass for that someone new to show up. I'm not attracted to just anyone and, as an INFJ, my attraction for someone has barely anything to do with looks or physical appearance. It might be instant, but it's not an external thing. It's an energetic connection, and when it happens, it goes deep.

Our society *is* starting to open up more, and to accept that love and sexuality do not come in a one-size-fits-all box but, instead, occur on a spectrum. However, we still have much to explore in this arena. As a weirdo eccentric, I've found that I don't do so well trying to adhere to rigid, traditional ideas about sexual connections, romantic relationships, or marriage. When I first began putting out feelers with my more conventional friends about falling in love with people who were not my spouse, I was quickly shut down. I got lectured and ignored, while at the same time feeling like I was triggering and angering my friends. It wasn't until I realized that those friends just weren't on my wavelength, and then pursuing new friends who had more fluid ideas about relationships, that I felt like I had found my place.

The best thing to do is also the hardest thing to do: Be honest about your desires when it comes to love. Let me tell you, I REALLY did not want to share the truth of my feelings with my husband. I was terrified he would be irrevocably hurt, or that he would leave me, or both. But there came a day when all the pretending I was doing stopped working. The masks I was so used to wearing crumbled and I had to take a chance. I'm so glad that I did.

Now, I'm able to welcome soul connections with people when they come into my life, and I'm not scared that I'm doing something wrong or that I'm betraying my most important relationship, my marriage. I'm able to accept that this is the way I am, this is the way I work, and this is what's best for me. On top of that, it's helped my relationship with my husband grow stronger because there is nothing in my heart that I'm hiding from him. As terrifying as it was, when I took off all my masks and he finally saw the real me, it was also a total relief.

This doesn't mean that there are no more challenges for me in the realm of love. I still get obsessed. I still get energetically overwhelmed by intense romantic feelings. I still get scared. But now I'm way more open to taking the ride with someone and seeing what happens. I've learned and grown more than I ever have before in my life.

The one thing I can say with certainty is that INFJ love is NOT for the faint of heart.

CHAPTER 9

Connection with Other Types: Accepting the Gifts of Different Personalities

A few years ago, in 2016, I wrote a blog post geared specifically toward INFJs that apparently still resonates today, because I still get emails about it. In the article, I talk about how INFJs can easily become obsessed with people and want to intimately bond with them, seemingly out of nowhere. I call this tendency, "the fascination." As in, "when the fascination hits me, I'm powerless to resist it."

This is how I've always experienced it, as a fascination with someone that overtakes me like a tidal wave. From the emails I've received from readers, I know this is also how many other INFJs experience it too. The first thing my readers usually express about the phenomenon, in fact, is an overwhelming relief that they are not alone. Up until they found my article, they assumed something was wrong with them, that maybe they had the potential to turn into a crazy stalker, but now they know they're just going through that thing that all INFJs go through at one point or another. That thing where we meet someone and want to crawl inside their head with them so bad it hurts.

The fascination is something that INFJs can't escape. However, from my own experience, it became much easier to manage after I discovered personality theory and all the different ways it can be applied to individuals. Before I knew anything about being an INFJ, I only knew that I was radically different from most other people and I had a burning desire to dissect the thoughts and feelings of others in an attempt to make sense of those differences. But I was constantly frustrated in my efforts because, at the bottom of it, I just didn't understand *why* we were so different. For example, as an emotionally-centered, service-oriented INFJ, coming face-to-face with an intellectually-centered, competition-oriented ESTJ left me confused and sometimes angry. I had similar reactions to many other types, but I had no system of knowledge to lead me out of the fog.

So, when I became fascinated with someone who—as I can see now in hindsight—was a very different personality type than me, my fascination took me to a place where I felt like I was banging my head against a wall. No matter what questions I asked or what information I was able to uncover about the person, the puzzle of how they worked remained unsolved. And an unsolvable puzzle of a person is possibly one of the most surefire ways to drive an INFJ absolutely crazy.

But this all changed when I learned more about personality theory. First, I dived into the Myers-Briggs Type Indicator® system and then I researched the Keirsey Temperament Sorter, and then I ended up studying archetypes and how they work within an individual's makeup. Every new piece I absorbed helped me to untangle the knots of the most difficult people to understand. Then, a very surprising thing happened. After I had saturated myself with what seemed like every bit of information on being an intuitive and what that meant and how rare it was and how so many other people would probably never understand me, a person who was my exact opposite in almost every way unexpectedly walked into my life and blew all my assumptions about personality to smithereens.

He was an ISTP.

We met because we started working together on a project, and so we were required to communicate with each other frequently. When the first symptoms of the fascination began showing up, I took it in stride. This had happened to me before when working with people closely, so it didn't seem to be out of the ordinary. I figured it would probably burn itself out in a week. But I was puzzled when the weeks came and went, and the fascination only grew. I then went from puzzled to astonished when I realized how strongly I felt connected to this person. After all, he was a thinker, *and* a sensor. Weren't the thinkers the people who had no patience for all my messy emotions? Weren't the sensors the people who would *never* understand me?

But I didn't feel that way around my ISTP friend. In fact, I felt so accepted and understood by him that I also felt safe enough to open up and share my true thoughts and feelings, a rare occurrence for me with anyone.

When I looked around online for more information to explain why I was clicking so well with my ISTP friend, I ran into a definite bias against sensors. According to many articles and forums, sensors were shallow and only lived in the moment. They had no interest in discussing deep topics like philosophy, spirituality, or metaphysics. They couldn't understand intuition and how it worked, and they didn't value it at all. I also ran across rants from feelers against thinkers (thinkers were cold and emotionless), and thinkers against feelers (feelers were overdramatic and self-absorbed).

However, as my friendship with a real-life ISTP continued, I found all these statements to be blatantly false.

Yes, my ISTP friend valued logic over intuition, but he still listened to me when I detailed my intuitive dreams to him. Yes, he preferred playing a game of soccer to reading a book, but he still asked me about my writing. And yes, his natural tendency was to live moment-to-moment, but he still let me know that I was an important person in his life and he wasn't going to forget about me when we stopped working together.

Perhaps most importantly, through my friendship with this ISTP, I realized how very similar we were in so many ways. In fact, I often joked with him about how we seemed to be the same personality "turned inside out." The INFJ's top two functions are introverted intuition and extraverted feeling; these are the third and fourth functions for the ISTP. Likewise, the ISTP's top two functions are introverted thinking and extraverted sensing; these are the third and fourth functions for the INFJ. So, we were able to somewhat easily meet in the middle on introverted thinking and introverted intuition.

When we got started talking about systems of ideas and how they applied to real-world situations, we could talk for hours.

Our "inside-outness" extended to other areas as well. One day, I told my ISTP friend that I tended to absorb other people's emotions and sometimes, after I had soaked up intense sorrow from someone else, I ended up needing to cry later in the day to release it out of my system. He carefully processed this information, then said he would make a mental rule not to ever tell me anything sad because apparently it would make me cry and he didn't want that. I was inordinately touched when he told me this because he was so earnest, and also because I saw in a flash how the rules he made for himself paralleled my own.

Instead of my rules applying to emotional situations, though, they tended more in the direction of helping me negotiate the world of physical objects. For instance, whenever I needed to handle anything to do with electronics at my office, I memorized the instructions and followed them so precisely that it was nearly impossible for me to extrapolate outside of that exact situation. So, I would memorize, "do not ever touch the blue wire," without grasping what the blue wire was or the reason for not touching it. Just like my ISTP friend memorized, "do not tell Lauren anything sad," without being able to extend the reason for that to any other set of circumstances.

When I thought about it, I realized that my ISTP friend and I both used the strategy of memorizing sets of rules—him around emotions and me around mechanical things—because these things fell into the category of our fourth functions, respectively. So, in layman's terms, he was at the level of a four-year-old child when it came to negotiating the emotions of others, and I was at that same level when it came to negotiating my way through the world of machines. Even though it seemed we were "inside out" when it came to the areas in which we were weakest, I thoroughly comprehended his motivations and why he used the memorization of rules as the best possible strategy.

Because I did the same thing.

My ISTP guy ended up becoming one of my very best friends. My relationship with him showed me that other intuitive feelers are not the only people who hold the potential to understand me, and vice versa. Each relationship with a different type is a different experience, with its own potential. To me, exploring another intuitive feeler is like diving into an ocean. They don't know what fully lies in their depths either, and it's not unusual to discover chasms and abysses that might be home to things that will break your mind wide open. As I explored my ISTP friend, I came to think of him as more like a mountain trail. It's easy to see what lies ahead, for a little way at least, but there are also twists and turns on the trail that lead to unexpected vistas.

I don't think it's any accident that the Myers-Briggs Type Indicator® has been around for quite some time but has also experienced a phenomenal surge in interest in the past few years. Our society has entered an age where the violence we have done to ourselves emotionally is finally catching up to us and demanding payment. Mass automation, manipulative technology, consumer culture, repressive political systems—all these things and more have been responsible for suffocating creativity, sexuality, spirituality, heart connection, and emotional exchange between human beings. We have painted ourselves into a corner, emotionally speaking, and now we can't see our way out of it. We are desperate for new ways of understanding each other and better ways of resolving our apparent differences.

Before learning about personality theory, I would have been fascinated by my ISTP guy, but I also would have ended up frustrated. I would have asked him countless questions, but not been able to get very far with his answers. I would have subconsciously assumed that somewhere, deep inside, he was just like me: emotional, sensitive, dreamy, irrational, and imaginative. I would have felt like he was holding back, hiding the ocean that I would have assumed existed twenty thousand leagues down deep inside him. I would have left every one of our interactions feeling dissatisfied, and misunderstood.

However, when I came to the relationship armed with the knowledge of all the different personalities and how they manifest in individuals, my interactions with my ISTP friend took on an entirely different hue. I wasn't frustrated with him, or at least, not for very long. I let go of my expectation that he was secretly just like me and hiding it. I was able to accept him for what he was—a beautiful mountain trail instead of a mysterious ocean—and I was able to have fun exploring that with him, instead of expecting him to be something different.

Because of my relationship with my ISTP friend, I revisited the MBTI system to learn more about him, and to remind myself of how I was wired, and accept that more fully too. I don't suggest that anyone invest in any certain theory of personality as THE answer to everything, but it is an important starting point for all people to begin to understand and accept themselves. A key element of this is continuing to learn about other types long after we've exhausted researching everything we can about our own, because the more we learn about ourselves and other people—the more open we are to exploring enigmatic oceans *and* interesting mountain trails alike—the more at home we will feel in the world, and the more at home we can make others feel too.

CHAPTER 10
INFJs as Growth-Oriented Individuals: Building a Community of Support

It was October in San Francisco, which meant Indian summer had come to the Bay Area, and it was my 40th birthday. I'd taken the day off work to drive down to Big Sur, that wild and rugged stretch of the California coastline where Jack Kerouac had an epic alcoholic nervous breakdown almost 60 years earlier. Every year I spent my birthday alone, by choice. For me, it was an opportunity to take inventory. Where had I been? And where was I going? I usually gravitated toward picking a spot on a secluded beach or deep in the hills. I needed to be in total solitude, not so much to think, but more to intuit what was going on deep inside me.

This year was no exception.

I ended up sitting on the side of a cliff, listening to the boom of the waves crashing into the rocks below and observing the sparkle of the sun on the water. The spot I had picked to sit and meditate this year wasn't as secluded as I would have liked, as tourists kept zooming up in cars and parking beside me, getting out for a couple minutes to take a selfie and then moving on. My seat was right at the edge of the cliff and I felt how easy it would have been for any one of those strangers to give me a good shove and send me over. As I thought about it more, I began to feel that my choice to continue sitting there could be used as an exercise in trusting humanity. I decided I was up to the challenge.

For the past couple of months before this, I'd been going through what I thought of as an "intense growth period." Of course, I was always growth-oriented, and had been my entire life. Even when I was only ten years old I was thinking about developing my character and what that really meant. I'd always been interested in the personal development of others too. I began naturally coaching my friends in different areas when I was in my teens. To me, the purpose of any human life was growth, and so that was what I was striving to do all the time.

But, every once in a while, I went through intense growth periods. I felt like I came out of these intense growth periods as an entirely new person. To move forward, I needed to step over the corpse of my past self.

One such period occurred when I was 15 years old. A deep inner shift had been stirring in me for months, and then one weekend I shoplifted for the first time on a Friday night, got drunk for the first time the next night, Saturday, and then lost my virginity Sunday afternoon. It was a lot to happen in three days, but I never felt out of control in any way. Instead, I felt like a slimy wet butterfly with wings still wrapped tightly to its body, pushing itself out of the chrysalis into the sun for the very first time. I was unsteady, yes, wobbly for sure, but I was also finally manifesting the changes that had been occurring internally for months; now they were happening on the external level, in the form of concrete physical actions.

The period of time around my 40th birthday was similar. I had just returned from a retreat for writers and artists in Santa Fe, and I'd also recently met someone new who had sparked my heart in just the right way. My sexual and creative energy was through the roof. I was bursting with new ideas and excitement for the future. I was looking forward to my 40s in a big way. My intuition was telling me that I was going to experience inner shifts on a scale I had never before seen. I couldn't wait.

However, I was also having flashbacks to when I was 15. Even though I understood what I was going through, it was difficult to explain to other people. For weeks leading up to my current intense growth period I swung back and forth between anxiety and euphoria. All I wanted was to take long walks by myself and think or go for long drives by myself and listen to music. Even though I was having a hard time sleeping, I felt grounded by a solid feeling of inner peace. Everything was changing, but at the same time, everything was going to be okay.

Before I knew that I was an INFJ, and fully grasped what being a growth-oriented person meant, I worried that something was wrong with me whenever I went through one of these intense growth periods. I wondered if I had symptoms of being bipolar, because each growth period came with its own feelings of dark despair paired with joyful euphoria. I also tended to make decisions that seemed questionable to others, like the shoplifting or sleeping with someone seemingly on a whim. But that was only on the surface. Deep inside I knew I was deliberately choosing fringe experiences—experiences outside of the mainstream that carried an emotional charge and the volatility of risk, but also demanded independent thought and critical thinking—for a very good reason.

Growth.

That was my whole reason, because that was the whole point of my life.

After I learned I was an INFJ, these intense growth periods started to make more sense, because I started talking to other INFJs who reported similar types of experiences. Not everyone was like me, of course. Each person's growth periods reflected their personality and the context of their life. I found that my growth periods tended to include moving outside the norms of society in some way, whether that meant taking psychedelics or having sex with someone totally new, no strings attached. But for some INFJs it meant suddenly leaving their old church and joining a new one. Or traveling alone to a foreign country they had never visited before. Or withdrawing completely from the world for a while and severing relationship connections that had been entrenched for years.

No matter what form the intense growth period took, it appeared that one thing was the same. The people in the INFJ's life, the ones who were observing it from the outside, didn't really understand what was going on or why. To them, it seemed simply like their INFJ had been one way and then suddenly, one day, they weren't that way any longer. Out of the blue, their INFJ was making abrupt changes without any sensible cause to do so, and when they tried to explain their reasons they still didn't make much sense.

That's because the key piece of the puzzle missing from this equation is the knowledge that, at the core, every INFJ is a growth-oriented individual.

I've talked to and met a lot of INFJs, and I am constantly surprised by the differences among our type. However, I can say there is one thing that holds true across the whole spectrum of INFJ individuals: every single one of us is growth-oriented. Although we may express ourselves in a variety of ways from INFJ to INFJ, we live with growth as our soul purpose, no matter what kind of life we choose.

This is not to say INFJs are the only growth-oriented people on earth. Any person can be growth-oriented, it all depends on the individual. Regardless of type, I believe that growth-oriented people all share a collection of the same traits, and it seems to me that these traits are rarely altered or modified during the course of our lives. Here's a basic list culled from my own experience, and my observation of others:

We have little to no hang-ups about age. If we find someone interesting we don't care if that person is much younger, or much older, than us. Likewise, we don't identify with our own age very strongly. We choose our activities, friends, and lifestyle according to passion instead of age bracket.

We tend to choose unconventional and challenging life experiences for ourselves that are hard for others to understand. We very rarely feel that we are a "victim" of these circumstances and, in fact, always secretly feel satisfied because we know we are learning from them.

We have a strong desire to learn how to move from being a purely reactive human being into a state of higher consciousness. We love to observe our own thoughts, triggers, and psychological patterns (as well as those of others) in an effort to uplevel ourselves mentally and emotionally.

We tend to struggle to fit in with the mainstream population in terms of aiming to accomplish external "life goals," such as climbing the career ladder, or gaining social status to impress others.

We have an acute desire to see that "life is a gift," instead of "life is hard." This desire influences the trajectory of our lives on a grand scale.

What can be most difficult for a growth-oriented person is when we are surrounded by other people who are not the same way. Now, it is perfectly okay not to be growth-oriented. I believe everyone has shown up in this life to work on different things and we need all sorts of different types of people in the world to make a beautiful whole. So, if someone in your life is not growth-oriented like you are, that doesn't mean you're better than them or that they need to get their shit together or something. It just means you two are different. But, it is important to take that difference into account when you're struggling with your own growth-oriented issues and trying to explain them to that person. Because the bottom line is: If they're not growth-oriented, they ain't gonna get it.

This is why it's so important to bring people who *are* growth-oriented into your life, especially if you're an INFJ. Because when you go through an intense growth period and start "acting crazy" to the rest of the world, your growth-oriented friends will get it. Also, even if you go into withdrawal mode and don't want to talk about it, at least you'll know there are other people out there like you, you're not crazy, and your life is not imploding for no reason. You're just growing.

Growth is hard. It's messy and painful and confusing. But you will come out on the other side better for it, always. For an INFJ, growth in this life is the most important thing we can do. If we're serious about living our best life, then we're going to have to jump off the high dive and get into the growth game.

For an INFJ, it's the only game there really is.

PART III

THE REVOLUTION IS HERE:

Using Our INFJ Power to Heal the World

CHAPTER 1

INFJs as Multipotentialites: Embracing Our Fire and Passion

I had just gotten an email from a new client, and as I read it over for the second time I inwardly sighed. The problem she was trying to describe was something I had seen before, many times. In fact, almost three quarters of my clients complained about the same issue. *Identifying* the problem wasn't hard; working through it was another story.

This client, like almost all my clients, was an INFJ. She had no lack of creative ideas she wanted to explore. No, in her case—as it is with so many INFJs and INFPs—she felt like she had too many.

This particular INFJ was passionate about peaceful parenting methods, drawing and illustration, Reiki, yoga, writing poetry, and using dance to heal the body. She wanted to read as many books as she could about all these topics and use the information to give birth to her own creative path. However, she had limited time. She was the mother of two small children and also worked as a teacher. In her email she said that she felt like her tendency to be pulled in so many creative directions was somehow wrong in itself. Didn't that mean she was scatterbrained, or flaky? Didn't she need to be focused and driven to ever accomplish anything?

The problem—as I knew from working with so many intuitives—was not that my client needed to narrow her focus. It was that she needed to accept herself for what she was and embrace the unique way that she worked. Unfortunately, this is easier said than done, because in our culture we are brought up to believe that the linear way of doing things is the best way of doing things.

Western society is made up mostly of sensors, 80 percent of the population is the approximate percentage. And honestly, it doesn't matter if it's 80 or 70 or 90 percent, the essential takeaway is that *most other people in our society are not intuitives.* So, the intuitive always finds herself in the minority, and always struggles against the generally accepted rules and systems of our society, most of the time never realizing that these rules and systems are so generally accepted precisely because they work for the sensors.

Most sensors tend to do very well working with a linear method. Even the more spontaneous sensor types like the ISTP and ESFP can get on board with a linear strategy relatively easily and make it work for them. The rational intuitives (the INTJ, INTP, ENTJ, and ENTP) can also potentially work well with linear methods because their minds have a strong analytical bent. They may jump all over the place with ideas, but most of the time they are still able to organize those ideas and build the actual project out in a linear way. INFJs and INFPs are an entirely different story. When we try to combine an overly rigid linear strategy with the naturally wild and fluid creativity of these two intuitive feeling types, we get a whole ton of resistance as the result, and that halts progress altogether.

This theory might seem weird and contradictory at first glance, because aren't INFJs super organized? Aren't we future-oriented and don't we plan ahead for everything? Yes, we are, and, yes, we do. But it's important to note that this organizing/planning/futurizing talent applies almost solely to the *externals* of an INFJ's life. Also, in my opinion, much of our obsessive planning is actually driven by anxiety at the root, rather than our natural talent for forecasting. So, it's very common to see a lot of INFJs who have a five-year plan, know exactly where they want to go in their career, are having lunch in two weeks with a friend and have already picked the restaurant, etc., and who use those details and deadlines as a way to feel in control. This might work as an anxiety-reduction strategy in the short term, but it only deals with the *external* pieces of the INFJ's life and those external pieces are worlds away from what is going on within the inner landscape of the INFJ, which is where every shred of our creative work is born.

When we attempt to use that same organizational talent to channel our internal creative energy in a linear way, it gets us nowhere. Then we end up creatively frustrated. The reality is that it is normal for INFJs and INFPs to experience our creative energy as chaotic and tumultuous. It is normal for us to be consumed by a million different desires. And, it is normal for us to attempt to use our planning skills to manage our messy and unpredictable creativity, and then fail epically because it appears that we simply cannot pick one thing and stick with it.

Fortunately, there are people out there who are working diligently to pioneer the idea that we don't have to adhere to a narrow straight line to be successful in life. Emilie Wapnick is one example of a leader in the field of creativity who recognizes that being passionate about many different creative pursuits can actually be a gift instead of a liability. Wapnick coined the word "multipotentialite," a term that immediately resonated with creatives when it began to show up on social media around 2010, finally giving a name to the highly creative person's experience of being driven by many different passions. Wapnick is a multipotentialite herself and the founder and creative director of puttylike.com, a website specifically created for multipotentialites.

Wapnick describes a multipotentialite in this way:

A multipotentialite is a person who has many different interests and creative pursuits in life.

Multipotentialites have no "one true calling" the way specialists do. Being a multipotentialite is our destiny. We have many paths and we pursue all of them, either sequentially or simultaneously (or both).

Multipotentialites thrive on learning, exploring, and mastering new skills. We are excellent at bringing disparate ideas together in creative ways. This makes us incredible innovators and problem solvers.

When it comes to new interests that emerge, our insatiable curiosity leads us to absorb everything we can get our hands on. As a result, we pick up new skills fast and tend to be a wealth of information.

I couldn't have described the temperament of a highly creative INFJ or INFP better myself. Wapnick's definition is perfect and her website is incredibly helpful too. By building an online resource for multipotentialites Wapnick has given all of us who struggle with the multipotentialite experience the knowledge to begin moving forward in a constructive way. But in order to begin moving forward, we INFJs and INFPs must stop fighting ourselves—and our natural tendencies—first. We can read Wapnick's definition and identify with it, and we may even rationally agree that having a lot of different passionate interests does not mean we are wrong in some way, but if we're still in a place of emotional resistance about it, then forward motion becomes much more difficult.

Emotional resistance almost always comes back to limiting beliefs, and it's easy to see where most of us got our limiting beliefs about devoting ourselves to a multitude of passions. With the rise of industrialization and automation in the twentieth century, routines, schedules, and rigid processes were lauded as THE way to do things. Our culture is a culture that has prided itself on being efficient, rational, and very, very productive for a long time. As a rule, mainstream society has not traditionally encouraged different ways of thinking or doing things outside of the linear box. However, the rise of the internet has ushered all of us into a world where a vast amount of information is available instantly, and people can work and connect with each other from anywhere, whether "anywhere" is a skyscraper in Tokyo or a beach in Mexico.

The linear method of starting from A, and then moving onto B and C, can be valuable, and people can still gain an advantage in some situations from being a specialist in one area only, but the truth that can't be ignored any longer is that—as a collective—we're shifting into new territory where we need people who are good at and interested in a lot of different things. We need these kinds of people to be passionate about all their different interests in order to tie them together to come up with innovative, creative solutions to the problems of the future that we never thought we would be confronted with or have to solve.

Problems like:

How are we going to feed all the billions of people on the planet, without depleting the planet's health and resources any more than we already have?

How are we going to apply the question of human rights to AI workers in the future?

How are we going to balance the masculine and feminine energies on the planet in a way that works for everyone?

These questions are just a sample. There are thousands more awaiting humanity as we embark on the next few centuries ahead of us. None of these problems are going to be solved with the same old ways of thinking, or by people who are "experts" in one area only.

If we feel that we *shouldn't* have a bazillion different interests, and that we *should* pursue only one narrow line of thought or inquiry in our lives, then we will always be slaves to this *should* and *shouldn't*. We will always stay stuck in that place we've been for so much of our lives, feeling out of step with the rest of society, feeling like the weirdo no one understands, feeling like we're wrong or not good enough or a freak in some way. That's where the creative blocks come in and start to do real damage. Because as soon as an INFJ or an INFP feels that "I'm-too-weird-and-will-never-amount-to-anything" feeling we start getting sucked into the black hole of low self-esteem.

Being a multipotentialite is inextricably intertwined with being a growth-oriented person, so it's important to use the same strategies for success when it comes to fostering a healthy relationship within ourselves and with others. Just as when we realize that we need other growth-oriented individuals in our lives, it's important to take the knowledge of being a multipotentialite and apply it to critically analyzing our social circle too. Every close relationship should bring something valuable to the table, that's first thing, and there should be at least one or two other people in our circle who share our multipotentialite nature. When we have people in our lives who are just as insatiably curious, intellectually voracious, and highly creative as we are, we won't feel so weird and like we don't belong. In fact, we'll start to blossom in ways we never thought possible.

This might seem hard to pull off, especially if you've spent years tolerating mostly one-sided relationships. It's easy for INFJs and INFPs to fall into one-sided relationships because it's natural for us to give without expecting anything in return, and also because it feels safe in a way. Being in a one-sided relationship means we don't have to be truly vulnerable with anyone, and we don't run the risk of being laughed at or misunderstood. We can securely play our role of constant listener, the person who always understands and never judges, and we know that the other person will almost always approve of us, as long as we don't stray outside of our prescribed role.

However, one-sided relationships are definitely *not* growth-oriented relationships, and they're also not very interesting to multipotentialites in the long run. Multipotentialite INFJs and INFPs are on fire to participate in the dance and drama of humanity and to suck the juice out of every interaction, positive or negative, that we have with our fellow humans. So, if you look around at your social circle—and you're ruthless in your analysis of what you find—and you discover that your social landscape suffers from the dead weight of too many one-sided relationships, it's time to get real about cutting some of these people out of your life.

You might get scared and start to panic about letting a bunch of people go, thinking you'll die old and abandoned and alone. But I promise you that new people will come in. INFJ and INFP multipotentialites contain a light that shines so bright and a life force so magnetic and attractive to others, we will never be at a loss for finding new relationships. The key is that we have to accept ourselves for who we are, *just as we are right now.*

Our brains take off in a thousand different directions every single day, that's just part of our package. As for our passions having no limits, well, that's just part of our destiny.

CHAPTER 2

The INFJ Intuitive Gift: A Different Way of Seeing the World

In 2018 I stumbled across a book that took me even further in my INFJ journey. The book was *The Way of the Human Being* by Calvin Luther Martin and I had initially picked it up because I'd been interested in the subject matter—Native American spirituality—for quite some time. The first few chapters pulled me in effortlessly, but when I began reading one chapter in particular I felt tears welling up in my eyes. The story the author shared resonated with me in a way that went far beyond intellectual engagement.

Martin described a meeting of the US Fish and Wildlife Department in Bethel Alaska, to which members of the local Native community (the Yupiit, the most numerous of the various Alaska Native groups) had been invited. The latter half of the meeting was focused on discussion of the dwindling moose population. At one point, one of the Yup'ik spoke up. He said the government officials should talk a bit more quietly because the moose could hear their words and "might take offense at what was being planned for them, possibly even disappearing altogether."

The author described how the government biologist paused for a moment in his speech but then went on discussing the matter as if no one had spoken at all. I wasn't there in the room that day, but still, I knew the biologist had heard what was said about the moose, he just chose to ignore it. I also knew that some of the other government officials in the room had most probably rolled their eyes.

Even if the author didn't say it, I knew what those officials had been thinking, and even if the officials themselves didn't say it, I knew the Yupiit people received the message loud and clear.

They had been dismissed.

The government officials couldn't hear what the Yup'ik man was trying to tell them because they were coming from a worldview that only included the concrete reality they were able to locate and recognize purely through their five senses. What the Yupiit people believed made no sense because the government officials had no point of reference for what they were trying to tell them. To the government officials, the Yup'ik man must have appeared to be stupid or crazy because, to them, it was just crazy talk, and they would be fools to take it seriously.

But I knew exactly what that man had been saying when he tried to warn the government biologist that the moose might overhear the conversation. No, the moose were not standing right outside the window listening in, but *energetically* they were present and *energetically* they were linked to the intentions and agenda of all the people sitting in the room that day, discussing the future of those moose. Of course. It seemed so obvious to me. How could the government officials not see that?

Part of me was left dismayed, shaking my head and puzzled over how something so clear could remain invisible to some people, but another part of me wasn't surprised at all. I had dealt with this same reaction from others all my life, and so I knew how the Yupiit people must have felt.

For as far back as I can remember, I have "gotten information" about people. I use the term "getting information" because I honestly have never known what to call it. It doesn't feel like piecing together a puzzle and coming to an *ah-ha* conclusion about someone, although that frequently happens too, and it's not noticing subtle hints that other people miss. It's *information*. It's clear, direct, and very detailed. It leaps into my mind all at once, fully formed. It's a kind of knowing that feels, unmistakably, like truth.

One time I saw that a new coworker—who I had barely exchanged five words with—had been sexually assaulted. I saw what she had been wearing the morning after the attack as she picked up the pieces.

Another time another coworker walked by me on the way to the restroom and I immediately knew she had gone through an abortion. Still another time, my husband mentioned a friend of his who was experiencing problems with his wife and I saw that she had been molested as a young girl, by her grandfather. It didn't matter that I barely knew these people, or had never met them at all, I just knew. And I knew that my knowledge was true.

Sometimes the information I receive is backed up by others, later, who confirm independently and unknowingly that what I saw is, in fact, true. Sometimes I never find out if it's true or not. I intuitively realized long ago that when I get information like this about someone it is sacred, and not to be shared with anyone else, ever.

It's not something I can control. I can't turn it on or shut it off. For years and years, I thought I was making things up, that my imagination was in overdrive. Once or twice I came across someone else like me. Someone else who saw things, sometimes, about the secret buried truths that lay in the off-limits regions of other people. Carefully, we shared our experiences, always tip-toeing around the subject. After all, it was crazy, wasn't it? *We* must be crazy.

But as I began to research Native American philosophy and spirituality, my reference points began to shift. I began to comprehend how heavily our society leans on the concrete, objective view of the world and how strongly that worldview was at odds with what I had experienced in my own life. Because, as I revisited and reexamined my psychic experiences, I realized that my visions didn't feel like magic, or like anything miraculous. It didn't feel at all like I had superpowers. It just felt like there was energy there, old energetic imprints left behind, and I could see them even if most other people couldn't.

But whenever I've tried to tell anyone about my psychic experiences, I have usually been met with the reaction the Yup'ik man got from the government officials. I have been dismissed. People have told me I was imagining things, or implied I was lying. Those who were a bit more diplomatic told me they were sure there was some rational explanation. They said I must be good at picking up on body language and the nuances of facial expressions. Or possibly someone mentioned something to me in the past and I forgot all about it and then conveniently remembered it at the right time, forgetting that I forgot about it in the first place. Or maybe I just really wanted to believe that I had some sort of psychic vision, because I've always been the dreamy poet type.

It's difficult to put into words how hurtful and heartbreaking every one of those statements felt when they were made to me. In fact, it was so incredibly painful to feel dismissed in that way, that I ended up closing myself off from a lot of people for a long time. Although I was able to get perspective on these experiences later, as I got older, it didn't change the pain I went through in the moment. Looking back and seeing that the person had obviously not been on my wavelength and the interaction was probably a learning experience for us both, didn't change the wounding I experienced around it. So, for a long time, I tried to shut down that intuitive "psychic" side of myself. It just seemed safest.

However, a few years after I got sober and started exploring the spiritual realm my psychic experiences came back. I began to receive information so frequently, and also see the energetic patterns behind things so strongly, that I couldn't run from it anymore. This was in 2008, when I still knew barely any other intuitive people besides my husband. A year or so later I discovered I was an INFJ and had the first inkling that my psychic gifts might be connected to my intuitive temperament. However, most of what I found online explained away the deeper side of intuition, suggesting the same reasons I had heard so often in the past: INFJs were just exceptionally skilled at reading body language and other emotional cues. It was that and nothing more.

But then, in 2013, I started coaching INFJ and INFP writers, and what they shared with me showed me that there *was* something more to it.

These people had gone through the same experiences as me. Almost every one of my INFJ and INFP clients "got information," like I did, although not always in the same manner. Some people saw images and others heard voices. Some people just knew. Many reported getting information not just about the past and/or current emotional situation of the people around them, but also about highly-charged emotional events in the future. One of my clients told me she'd had intense dreams of burning buildings in the days leading up to 9/11. Another one of my clients told me she saw the events of 9/11 unfold in her mind exactly as they happened in real life weeks before everything occurred. She ended up sobbing on the phone with me, still devastated and carrying massive guilt about her vision.

I've never seen anything from the future before it happened, but I don't doubt either of those people one bit. I talked to both women many times and can confirm that each one was an absolutely sane, rational, and grounded person.

Both were also INFJs.

I don't know exactly how the intuitive gift works for INFJs and INFPs, but I do have a theory about it. If everything in the universe is made of energy, then I would guess that different waves of energy tend to sync up and amplify the frequency of whatever those waves are carrying. It seems that INFJs and INFPs are born with the ability to access energetic frequencies much more easily than the rest of the population. When energy syncs up and amplifies, we *feel* it, most especially when it's *emotional* energy, and this helps us tune in. When we tune in, we get information.

I don't know the science behind it, but that there *is* science behind it, I have no doubt. Our world just hasn't discovered it yet. Which leaves INFJs and INFPs in the unfortunate current situation of either feeling like we're crazy, or feeling like we're totally sane but misunderstood and rejected by society at large.

However, just as my little world changed when I connected with other INFJs and INFPs through my writing and my coaching business, the INFJ movement is now changing the larger world as it brings us all together. For the first time ever in history, we are all beginning to talk to each other and compare notes. What we're finding isn't just life changing, it's paradigm shattering.

Suddenly, we're not the only crazy one in the room anymore, and when we realize we're not alone, it doesn't matter if others dismiss our gifts. Because when we have each other we're not so focused on the wounding of the past. Instead, we can see exactly where we need to go, together, in the future.

CHAPTER 3

INFJs as Natural Mystics: Traveling Within to Bring Light out of the Darkness

It was a normal day at the office for me, which meant that a lot was going on. I'd had the same day job for eight years, and it had been relatively uneventful until this year, when the management changed. The company culture had changed too, and the new style included more happy hours, more company lunches, and more socializing in general. I'd spent most of the week engaged in a lot of chit-chat in big groups and deeper conversations with other coworkers that took place one-on-one. On this day, a small group had congregated near my desk and before I even realized what was happening, I went into energy overload. I felt shaky and weird, slightly manic, but also physically fatigued.

As soon as I could, I broke free from the office and walked across the street to the library, my safe haven. I tried to curl up in a corner and read my book, but I couldn't concentrate. I knew that I was experiencing the symptoms of being a stressed-out introvert, by now they were quite familiar, and I had no problem recognizing them when they occurred. But this was something different, something more. I was tired, but also amped up. I felt like I was bursting with energy, but at the same time like all that energy was about to fry my system. Now that I thought about it, I'd been feeling this way for days. In fact, I realized now, too, that I could recall going through cycles of this same feeling in the past.

It usually happened when I was working closely with a group of people, and that group was going through big changes. So, it had happened to me a lot when I was working at my first two crazy startups. At first, the manic feeling came on slowly. My energy increased every day until I was routinely skipping meals and waking up earlier and earlier in the morning. It felt good, for a while, until I started to feel the symptoms of burnout. At the end, before I hit the wall, I felt like I was a machine running purely on coffee and willpower. Then my battery died.

On this day in particular, I decided to do something different. Knowing now that I was an INFJ and an empath, I slowed down and took some time to check in with myself.

I sat in my corner seat at the library, put my hand over my heart, and felt into my energy system. I saw that a lot of new information had come to light recently that concerned my team of coworkers and all the changes that had occurred. Enough of the pieces had surfaced that they had begun to coalesce into a pattern. That was the problem. I wasn't just stressed out from not getting enough introvert time. I felt overwhelmed by the pattern coming together in front of me. I could see where my team of coworkers had been, and now, very clearly, where we were going.

On top of this, there was a high level of emotional energy in my office. The changes we had experienced hadn't been small. All of us had gone through an emotional blender over the past year. Raw feelings were still floating around—sorrow, anger, resentment, and fear. Fortunately, I could also feel that the first glimmers of hopeful enthusiasm were returning to the staff. Zooming in from the big picture, I could see that each person in my office was growing and evolving in a different way as a result of the recent changes. Each person's growth formed its own coalescence of pattern, too, and these individual patterns added to the pattern as a whole.

All this energy and the kaleidoscope of various patterns had come together, inside my one little mind and heart and soul. No wonder I felt like a freaked-out cat who couldn't stop yowling and trembling, and who wanted to do nothing more than hide under the bed.

I sat with this for a few minutes and then my body pulled me in the direction I needed to go. I found myself getting up and strolling through the aisles until I reached the very back shelves, the quietest spot in the building, where all the poetry books were kept. As I walked by, I followed my urge to put my hand on different volumes, lifting them out and paging through them as they called to me.

I read Walt Whitman and Sylvia Plath and felt my body beginning to settle. I read Adrienne Rich and felt myself center firmly back into my own energetic core. I moved onto the Beats and read Jack Kerouac and Allen Ginsberg and felt my mind and soul begin to clear. I moved through book after book, reading about artists who'd had visions and visionaries who made art, reading the words of others who had gone before me and been drawn down their own paths by the same things that drew me down mine—love, healing, compassion, wisdom, and the possibility of accessing a higher consciousness.

For a little while, with the help of those books of poetry, I was able to see reality for what it truly was: one big playful game full of possibility and magic. I was able to dive into my own soul and draw sustenance from it.

For me, submerging myself in creative beauty is akin to mystical contemplation. No, I wasn't communing with a god that belonged to any particular religion, but I was communing with what, to me, *is* God. By immersing myself in the energy and magic of artists who had gone before me in the past, I was able to steady my own little candle flame and reconnect it to the source of all light in the present.

My form of mystical contemplation also includes the distinct feeling of moving outside of this concrete reality. It's not anything like astral projection because I'm still here, inside my physical body, but my mind is able to move beyond boundaries and visit other realms. Sometimes it doesn't feel like much more than seeing a virtual reality through Walt Whitman's eyes, but I have had stronger, and stranger, experiences in the past where I felt like I actually traveled to another time or place. Somewhere distinctly "elsewhere" than the reality I inhabit from day to day.

I think all INFJs have this gift of being able to pop in and out of different realities at will, but many of us don't know we can do it, and when we find out that we can do it, we still don't know why. Similarly, the mystics have been the people throughout history who have cultivated the ability to go "somewhere else." This might be deep inside themselves or—who knows—maybe even into parallel universes, but wherever they journey, they return with what they've gathered there to help the rest of humanity and be in service in whatever way they can.

Being able to step outside of concrete reality can be an invaluable tool, because if none of us ever step outside of it we begin to believe that it's all deadly, seriously real. That it makes rational sense to hold venomous grudges against people and lay awake at night worrying about credit card debt. That it's normal to feel constantly scared and stressed by the media and the unpredictability of world events. But those of us who are mystically inclined have the potential to be the true voices of reason in our society, despite the perpetual tumult going on around us, and in order to see with complete clarity, we need to not only think outside the box, but sometimes, leave it altogether.

Leaving the box is more difficult than it sounds. We are a culture ruled by rationality with science as our modern-day religion. Yes, I do believe science is incredibly valuable and a sacred kind of work all its own, but it's only one side of the conversation. We have become so focused on what is concrete and tangible, so concentrated on only what we can prove and what we can interpret through our five senses, that as a society we have cut off part of our vision and blinded ourselves. But INFJs are gifted with introverted intuition as our dominant function, and this is a function that moves way beyond the five senses. It is the tool that allows us to leave the concrete, collective reality that surrounds us, at will, and with only the help of something as small as a poem, or a prayer.

I believe INFJs and INFPs are people who are natural mystics, meaning we are born with a temperament that pushes us to constantly seek connection with something higher than ourselves. We can also place our energetic fingertips on the spiritual pulse of people, whether in groups or at the individual level, and gauge what can be done to initiate healing. When we tap into energetic patterns like this—and reveal the possibility of healing to others—we shine a light that leads the way forward, even when it appears that our world, or an individual's life, is wrapped in the darkest chaos. This is why I believe the greatest mystics in the history of the world were also probably INFJs or INFPs, because the mystic exists to bring light out of the darkness.

Of course, INFJs and INFPs don't usually embrace the role of mystic. Many people view mystics as downright weird, and no one wants to be labeled as a religious nut, or "kooky" or crazy, or even just plain foolish. When we begin to talk about exploring our inner landscape as if it's a real, physical environment that we can walk around in and bring things back from, it's likely that most other people are just not going to understand this type of subject matter. But if we're serious about reaching our potential as INFJs and INFPs, we can't push our mystical tendencies away. The only way to self-actualize into our best selves is by fully welcoming *all* our abilities and strengths, even if those gifts are not understood, or might even be alarming, to the rest of the population.

Also, you don't have to be religious at all to explore mysticism. Creating art is an almost guaranteed gateway into exploring other realms and connecting with your higher power, whatever that may be. Many INFJs and INFPs are writers, which is one form of art that can take us deep inside ourselves or transport us to other places, but others of us are painters, sculptors, dancers, or musicians. The "flow state" that so many researchers have found evidence of people entering when completely engaged in a creative act can definitely be used as a form of communion with the creative heart of the Universe. The flow state is connection, at the deepest level. It is truth, in its purest form.

This is also one of the main reasons, in my opinion, that INFJs and INFPs are the healthiest when they are consistently creating art. Making art is a connection to Source, and communion with whatever, to us, is God, is something we need in our lives in order to feel fully alive. Exploring our inner landscape, transporting information from other realities into this one, drawing nourishment from the realm of the soul—these are all non-negotiables when it comes to maintaining a balanced state of health for the INFJ or INFP.

For INFJs and INFPs, our highest and best selves will emerge when we are both creating art AND diving deep into the well of our own soul. It is possible to do both at the same time. We don't need to be experts at meditation or a master of our artistic craft to bring out our inner mystic. We only need to begin to trust ourselves, and to be brave enough to forge on through the darkness, of which there will be plenty.

That day at the library, when I was feeling so overwhelmed and emotionally zapped, I was able to tap into my inner mystic and regain my balance. By moving outside this concrete reality and reconnecting with Spirit through the words of my fellow poets I was able to make sense of the tidal waves of energy crashing over me. The patterns I was desperately trying to organize finished their coalescence in my mind and finally let me rest. That was when I was able to return to my office with the clarity and wisdom I needed to help my coworkers.

As an INFJ, the only way I could get there was not by thinking outside the box, but by leaving it altogether.

CHAPTER 4

INFJs as Nonconformists: "Not Fitting In" Is Exactly What We're Here to Do

In the spring of 2010 I was living in San Francisco and working at my third startup. I'd had a rollercoaster of a ride since 2007, when I had first stumbled into the startup world and realized this fascinating space seemed to be made almost perfectly for me. Once I understood what startups—*my* kind of startups—had to offer, I was hooked, and it felt like there was no going back.

My kind of startup was small, 12 people or less. And it was new. I wanted to work at companies that had only been in business two or three years. I looked for companies that had a big vision, super passionate people, but no real infrastructure. I wanted the companies that still needed an HR department built from the ground up and had no official processes in place yet. When I walked into my third startup, and saw they didn't even have a water cooler, I knew I had found exactly what I was looking for.

When I told other people about the kind of startup I liked, most looked at me like I was crazy. I understood that look. It did seem that I was willing to work for companies that sometimes couldn't offer health insurance, and never offered dental, or that sometimes had to cut my salary when money was tight, or close to running out. But what I got back was so valuable that I was willing to put up with all that.

Because what I got back was freedom.

At these kinds of startups, I could make my own schedule. I could come to work at 6:00am or 10:00am, as long as I got what needed to be done, done. I could build my own desk and cram it into any random corner of the house or office we were working out of at the moment. I usually had a job title, but my title never really mattered. My bosses welcomed me jumping into other work activities that I wasn't qualified for in the least. I wanted to try my hand at taking tech support calls? Sure. I wanted to see if I could manage a PR list and contact reporters to do stories on us? Go for it. I had a crazy new idea for how we should market the latest changes to our website? Let's hear 'em.

Because there was so little structure, and because whatever structure existed was so new, everything was still porous and fluid. There was a ton of space and possibility. I could be extreme and creative and challenge myself at every turn.

To me, this was worth going without a water cooler and dental insurance.

I noticed something else during these years of working at lean, bootstrapped startups. These little crazy companies seemed to attract other people like me. People who were eccentric, fiercely self-sufficient, and wildly independent. People who loved taking chances. People who didn't just think outside the box but turned the box into a big origami frog and painted it pink with silver polka dots.

By the time I got to my third startup though, I was a little road weary of just *how* intense these companies could get. I was 32 years old and starting to think that maybe having reliable health insurance was something I should pay more attention to. My third startup combined my established needs for freedom, space, and independence with my newly burgeoning needs of reliability and a certain level of security. It was still a startup and it was still small, but there was very little turnover and there was a low risk of the company running out of money. My intuition told me that the owner and CEO knew exactly what he was doing. He had a solid plan and I knew that plan would succeed.

Six years later my intuition turned out to be right. The company was successful and the owner sold it to a bigger company. Then that company got acquired by someone even larger. So now we were owned by a huge corporation, a business that had locations all over the United States and a giant central campus too.

Within the first week under new ownership my intuition kicked in again. Changes were coming.

I had never before worked for a big corporation, but I almost immediately hated it. We all had to be on the same laptop and use the same office furniture. Alarms were installed on the doors and we all had to carry official badges to get in and out, even just to use the bathroom. There were now checklists and goal lists and performance reviews and required training in company culture, a course all employees had to complete to get on board with the team spirit of the company.

It sounded like indoctrination to me.

Then I noticed another pattern. After we became a corporation, we started attracting a different kind of person. A more average, conformist, submissive kind of person. It was about this time that I began to have an almost allergic reaction to the new environment, while one by one, all the people around me seemed to be conforming a little more each day to the new culture.

That's when I really got to thinking about the difference between me, and my coworkers.

As so many things do, it appeared to come back to me being an INFJ.

Out of all the types, in my experience, it's the INFJs, INFPs, INTJs, and INTPs (and sometimes the ISTPs) who display the strongest energetic independence from others, and consequently the strongest tendency to be nonconformists. I know that might sound harsh on the other types, but I believe it's true. And when I say "energetic independence from others" I don't mean that we don't need people or that we don't love people. I mean that we are somehow able to stay centered in our own individual energy system, even when everyone around us has fallen in line with a larger external energy system.

In my opinion, this is a matter of entraining, and I mean that in the zoological sense of the definition:

To adjust (an internal rhythm of an organism) so that it synchronizes with an external cycle, such as that of light and dark.

It was like the people at my company had slowly been absorbed into the new corporate system and that new system had an energy of its own. The energy was rigid, structured, dominant, competitive, and ultimately rooted in fear. *Belonging to the group* was valued far more highly than *creativity of the individual.* When my coworkers were exposed to enough of this energy over a long enough period of time, they slowly became entrained to it. Eventually, that corporate energy was what directed their thoughts and actions.

But, this never happened to me. It just didn't take. It was like I had some sort of force field around me and the corporate energy bounced right off it.

What was even more interesting was comparing how I entrained with individuals, as opposed to the larger collective. *That* I could do very easily, and almost to a fault. I immediately tuned in to the thoughts and emotions of others, and had done so my entire life. If I was around a person long enough, say for a whole weekend, I came away feeling saturated by that person, able to see every detail of the world through their eyes. This was hard for me. For many years I had difficulty understanding where my emotions ended and another person's began. If I became involved in someone else's crisis or drama it was like I fell into a black hole that was made up of this other person, and I couldn't crawl out again.

So, it wasn't that I was immune to *all* entraining. It seemed that I was particularly susceptible to entraining with others on a one-on-one basis, but entraining with a large group had little to no effect on me. And it seemed to be the other way around for everyone else. Most other people seemed to entrain very easily with large groups—teams and corporations and so on—but not so easily with other individuals.

I still don't have all the answers to these questions. I'm not a neuroscientist and I haven't done any official research. But my gut tells me that intuitive introverts—the INFJs, INFPs, INTJs, and INTPs—are born different, and that difference includes an odd immunity to group entraining while at the same time an odd susceptibility to one-on-one forms of entraining. For INFJs and INFPs the one-on-one obviously comes back to people and emotions. For the INTJs and the INTPs I've noticed that they seem to be able to entrain easily with the energy of ideas and systems, not just figuring them out but entering into them with a sense of communion.

So, why is this something that INFJs and INFPs need to be aware of and pay attention to, now more than ever?

Our world is in an intense transition state, and much of that transition is centered around technology. We have a lot of technology at our disposal, but a limited level of love to balance it. With the rise of social media, the online world has become a place where people are villainized, slandered, bullied, attacked, and destroyed every hour. This is mob energy, and a mob is nothing more than a violent collective of people. Similarly, there are movements of people active all around the world that are focused on hatred, vengeance, and destruction. Again, these movements are violent collectives. For those who are susceptible to entraining with large groups, and who already feel disempowered and victimized, it's all too easy to fall into one of these violent collectives.

This is why the unique makeup of INFJs and INFPs is so valuable. Because we have this very weird mix of somehow being immune to entraining with large collectives (like corporations), while at the same time easily entraining with just one other individual (like a reader), anything we put out into the world with a positive message has the potential to strongly influence others for the good. If you write a blog, or publish a book, or create music, or teach online courses, or do any of a hundred other things that enables you to form your light and love into an energy packet that you can make available on the internet, then you have the power to plant the seeds of positive change in someone else, anywhere across the world. If you choose instead to work as a therapist or counselor, or a nurse or teacher, in real time, you also have the power to entrain with others, to look inside them and see their emotions and their pain and help shift that energy in a positive way.

Because that's something else I've noticed: When we entrain with just one other individual, *they entrain with us too.* I believe this is why INFJs and INFPs make such amazing counselors. Our gifts in this area are rooted in our ability to easily enter into an energetic exchange with another. So, not only do we see and feel what they see and feel, but they are also able to enter our energetic space, and to choose to shift their frequency to a higher vibration as they sync with us. INFJs and INFPs have the ability to make others see their own future potential, *as if it is already real.*

My observations about how INFJs and INFPs entrain with others lead me to believe that it's just another case of how our temperament appears to endow us with wiring that is the opposite of what is found in most other people. But this opposite wiring exists for a reason. If we have the courage to own what we are and fully tap into it, there's no telling what a profound impact we could have on the world.

CHAPTER 5
The Potential of INFJ Creativity: Balancing Power with Love

When I was in college I had a friend whose parents used to be extreme anti-establishment hippies. They even had a copy of *The Anarchist Cookbook*, she told me in a conspiratorial tone one night when we were up late studying. *What's that?* I asked. *It's this manual for terrorists*, she said. *It's all about how to build bombs and turn guns into grenade launchers and a bunch of other crazy shit.*

Then we went back to studying and I forgot all about it until almost 20 years later when I found a random documentary that looked interesting on Netflix. *American Anarchist* was the name of it and when I read the description, that long-ago late-night conversation I'd had with my college friend came back to me.

When I watched the documentary I was astonished. Yes, *The Anarchist Cookbook* was a sort of manual for terrorists, but the guy who wrote it couldn't be farther from someone who would be involved in any kind of violence. His name was William Powell and he had written the book when he was 19 years old and living in the thick of late 1960s New York City, working at a counterculture bookstore by day and involved in protests by night. After writing the book, he'd moved on to a different phase of his life and tried to forget about it as much as possible. He became a teacher and advocate for kids with learning disabilities and worked for years in the Middle East and Africa, contributing to programs to help kids thrive, no matter what they struggled with on the learning front.

When the filmmaker confronted him with all the violent events that *The Anarchist Cookbook* had been linked to—school shootings, the big movie theater shooting in Colorado, plane hijackings—Powell said he was shocked, and heartbroken. He had been somewhat successful at avoiding ever thinking about the book for years, but now it had come back to haunt him, yet again.

What I found most intriguing was William Powell's past. He'd been raised partly in England, partly in the United States, and felt like an outsider in both places. He said no matter which country he was in at the moment the kids made fun of his accent and bullied him. His father was controlling and had extremely high expectations of him academically, which he couldn't meet. When he was in his early teens he was sent away to boarding school and molested by a person in authority there.

So, at the age of 19, when he found himself in the middle of all the chaos of the 1960s in New York City, he was already a very lonely, angry, victimized young man. He said he didn't even have to think about writing the book. The idea came to him suddenly and he followed it. He went to the New York Public Library and gathered all the information he needed from military manuals, and then he supplemented the "recipes" with his own thoughts on violent revolution. He said the book only took him three to four months to write and then he immediately found a publisher.

I wasn't surprised that he said the book seemed to almost write itself, and that a publisher instantly snapped it up. I believe that every book has its own energy stamp. Some are strong, some are a bit weaker, but every book has one. It's the energetic imprint of the author at the time of writing. This is why I tell my clients that no two authors can ever produce the same work, because every piece of writing produced has the energetic fingerprints of the author all over it, and every set of human fingerprints—in the tangible world or intangible—is unique.

When William Powell sat down to write *The Anarchist Cookbook* he tapped into the deepest recesses of his own pain, shame, anger, and violent longings. It was very likely that the resentment against his father and the man who sexually assaulted him, among others, had been festering for years. Added to that was his surrounding environment—

late 1960s New York City—which was saturated with chaos, conflict, and aggression. So, he was carrying a strong dark energy charge already, and then living within a collective that was carrying a similar charge. And, he was a writer. A thoughtful, intelligent, sensitive writer.

It's no wonder *The Anarchist Cookbook* was so easy for him to write, and then so easy to distribute.

It's also no wonder that, decades later, disturbed young people with violent tendencies gravitate toward the book. The book carries the exact same charge of dark energy that they do. Anger, resentment, hatred, and fear—specifically aimed at parents and other authority figures. The book *feels* right to them, on a very deep level.

We are living in a time in history when the dark energy charge is very high. So high, in fact, that many people are in despair about it. Along with the despair comes fear, naturally, which only feeds the dark energy. It's my thinking that this dark energy charge is so intense at this time because we've reached a point in our society where we have a significant amount of technological tools, a lot of power, so to speak, but we're still emotionally primitive in many ways, and so we don't have the level of love necessary to balance out all the new forms of power that have suddenly dropped into the lap of the human race.

When you have a high level of power combined with very little love you get something like Nazi Germany. Or Darth Vader and the Empire trying to take over the whole universe.

All this new technology we've created has brought obvious problems, like the now-heightened ability of one individual to commit mass violence relatively easily, cyberbullying and online shaming, and the streaming of violent acts on social media. But it's also brought us amazing new possibilities too, like the option for people to write and publish books entirely on their own, and the power to build our own platforms with a positive message and be seen and heard by an unlimited amount of people across the globe. As mentioned in the previous chapter, because INFJs and INFPs are so skillful at entraining with others one-on-one, any "energy packet" we put online for other people to consume has the power to shift individuals at a fundamental level. Thankfully, we can take advantage of this ability to use technology as a force of good.

When we choose to use technology as a force of good we achieve power *balanced with* love, and that's when we get something like Gandhi, instead of the Nazis. And instead of Darth Vader, we get the Jedi Knights, people who strive to take personal responsibility, act with honor, and respect life in all its forms.

I do believe INFJs and INFPs have some sort of inborn collection of traits that make us predisposed to be Jedi Knights. However, just like Luke Skywalker, many of us don't understand our Jedi Knight potential for a long time. We just know that we're different or weird, that maybe we're too sensitive or something. Even after we learn all about Highly Sensitive People and empaths and different personality systems, there is still something more, a deeper piece that we can't see but that we can *feel*. I know this from my own experience, but also because I've gotten hundreds of emails from INFJs and INFPs that all say the same thing. *I know I'm meant to do great things for the world, but I don't understand what. I know I was born to help people, but I don't know how. I know I can make the world a better place, but I don't know where to start.*

One guy who felt angry, alone, and afraid wrote a dark-energy book over 40 years ago that still speaks to those who carry that same dark energy. Doesn't it stand to reason that YOU could write a book today that carries an energy full of love that will still speak to those who need it years down the road?

William Powell channeled all his rage, pain, and shame and turned it against the critical voices and enemies that lived inside his head—his father, the man who molested him, and anyone in authority. He used the writing of his book as a way to aim for vengeance. He was trying to take his power back by evening the score. It wasn't until later in life that he found a better way to heal. He reached back down inside himself, into those hurt, dark places, and he used what he found there to reach out to others who were struggling just like he had in the past. That's when he became the great teacher who was such a positive force of good for kids with learning disabilities, kids who felt misunderstood, alienated, and alone. That's when he was able to build something out of his life that lifted those kids up and made a real, positive difference.

We can all take a lesson from his journey.

If you are an INFJ or an INFP, the chances are high that you've already gone through something in your life that injured you in a way that wasn't easy to heal. All people have gone through things like this, but I believe INFJs and INFPs are wired in such a way that we automatically turn inward when traumatized, sometimes for years, in an effort to make sense of the event and to find the pattern and deeper, emotional meaning in it. It's when we reemerge back into the external world from our inner recesses that we have to make our Darth Vader versus Luke Skywalker choice.

What are we going to do with the feelings that still haunt us from the traumatic event that changed us so profoundly? As an insanely high number of INFJs and INFPs are writers, the most frequent decision is to write about it in some form, whether that comes out as a book or a blog or a daily journal practice. We now also live in a world that comes equipped with all these new technological possibilities. We can broadcast our writing to everyone else on the planet. We can look inside ourselves, find all our pain, our fear, our anger, and yes, even our hatred, and we can contain it on the page. We can create an energy packet that is just waiting to be opened by anyone who stumbles across it.

So, what is your choice going to be? You may think you haven't made a choice yet, because your work is still sitting there inside you. You might be too afraid to start or not confident enough to believe you have anything worthwhile to share with the world. But *not* sharing your story, *not* actively using your own wounds to help others who are currently in the same boat, *is* a choice. Because you can bet there are plenty of people out there right now just like the guy who wrote *The Anarchist Cookbook*. There are plenty of people—many of them INFJs or INFPs just like you—who haven't yet reached a place of healing and are making the choice instead to distribute their dark energy packets to the world, little packets of poison just waiting for someone to open them up.

So, even if you don't feel confident, even if you're not sure where to start or what you want to say, your voice does matter. We need every single INFJ and INFP to begin creating whatever it is that wants to come out of our souls, and to use those creations for the good of humanity.

That's when we'll get to power *balanced with* love, and that's when we'll begin the journey toward real healing.

CHAPTER 6

INFJs as Entrepreneurs: Shifting into a Self-Employed Mindset

My junior year in college I attended a panel discussion for English majors. It took place in April of that year, and so the room was packed with a lot of other English majors who were also preparing to go into their senior year in the fall and starting to think seriously about career options. The panel was made up of four people who had majored in English at my university and who were now in their 30s and apparently had gone on to have successful careers using their English degrees. All four of them seemed ancient to my 20-year-old self as they delivered their stories with a slightly apologetic, yet hopeful, tone. Underneath their words, I could feel the truth. *Even though everyone thinks you're wasting your college education it's okay! You can be an English major and still actually become gainfully employed!*

One of the four was a teacher, one a lawyer, and I can't remember the other two, although I think maybe one of them sold life insurance policies. None of them inspired me in any way. It seemed like they had taken jobs just to pay the bills and were now dutifully doing their best to convince young college students that the life of a full-time employee was halfway decent.

This did not make me doubt my choice of major, however. Literature was my first love and I was rock solid in my decision to use my four years at college to devote myself to the study of it. I didn't have much in the way of a plan after that. I was kicking around the idea of waitressing for a while, but that was it.

Fast forward 20 years later to my current life, in which I am an author, a speaker, a coach, a teacher, and an entrepreneur. In this current life, just a week or so ago, I had a dream that I was back at college. I was frantically trying to find the English department so that I could sign up for classes, but I was blocked at every turn. And then, halfway through the dream, I realized that I didn't even really want to find the English department. I wanted to study business, instead.

I didn't have to work very hard to interpret this dream. Although I did make good on my promise to find work as a waitress right after graduation, I quickly moved on from that to a variety of different jobs. In 2007 I landed at my first startup and was hooked. The people I met in the startup scene in Seattle and San Francisco were worlds away from the people who had given me my idea of "business" as I was growing up in the Midwest. The startup people weren't like stodgy bankers or pretentious Wall Street guys. Instead, they were young, casual, and very creative. They weren't trying to build companies that fit the old model. In fact, the old model bored them. They wanted to do something totally new.

I fit right in to the startup world, although a few years had to pass before I figured out the reasons why. The answers slowly came as each startup I worked at grew larger and turned into more of a "real company." Something happened to the environment, the staff, and the culture after we hit about the 12-person mark in hiring. Official policies were put into place and then we needed an HR person. There were now more rules, and less self-sufficiency.

As I looked closer, I realized this was because very small lean startups attract one kind of person, and established companies attract another.

Under 12 people and the startup could still be considered similar to something like the Wild West. Gamblers, eccentrics, highly creative people, and those with a self-employed mindset thrived. After 12 people and we started getting into different territory. When we began turning into a legit company, we started attracting people who were more security-oriented and who were mostly driven by salary, benefits, and the status of a job title. These people had an employee mindset. They wanted someone else to set the rules, tell them what to do, and then follow that structure.

I discovered this division between the self-employed versus employee mindset by reading Robert Kiyosaki's brilliant book, *Rich Dad Poor Dad*. This book was recommended to me constantly by customers during the four years I worked at a bookstore, but I had too much resistance to anything that had to do with business to give it a chance. It wasn't until many years later when I had launched my own side hustle that I finally picked it up.

As I devoured Kiyosaki's book I realized why I had never been interested in business when I was young, but now, when I was in my mid-30s, I couldn't get enough of it. It was because now we were living in a new age, a time when the internet had changed everything, and business was radically different than what it had been before. Now, for someone to go into business, they didn't need to have a degree, get funding, understand complex accounting practices, or be prepared to hire and manage a staff. In our current world, anyone can be an entrepreneur and a business owner, and the only thing you really need is a creative mind and a laptop.

I saw that, in our current world, it's possible for me to have a self-employed mindset, be eccentric, highly creative, have a little bit of the gambler inside, go into business and be successful at it, *and still be me.*

And rest assured, I am not the only one who has discovered this beautiful fact.

Today's economy is slowly but surely moving from business being centered around old behemoth corporate beasts to lighter and faster freelancers, entrepreneurs, and side-hustlers that make up the more fluid gig economy. Now, I'm not saying that corporations are dead, or going anywhere anytime soon. But the new element is here to stay for the foreseeable future, and this new element gives INFJs and INFPs an advantage that we've never had before.

It's my feeling that a lot of INFJs and INFPs are like me, choosing to study something artistic or something that speaks to their heart, or both, as a career path. I also suspect that, like me, most INFJs and INFPs possess a high level of independence and fall clearly on the side of the self-employed mindset because of it. In addition, it seems most of us have shied away from anything business-related in the past because it feels conformist, maybe a bit cold, and also just not that interesting. But in this new world, where we can start our own businesses easily and online, and not be bothered with having to schmooze at business lunches to get ahead, well, the possibilities for highly creative INFJs and INFPs to find their calling through entrepreneurship are endless.

In fact, the unique gifts of the INFJ and INFP can even be an unexpected advantage when it comes to entrepreneurship. Since INFJs possess the dominant function of introverted intuition and INFPs the auxiliary function of extraverted intuition, both types are fantastic at identifying patterns that others cannot see, with the INFJ being especially good at forecasting predictions based on those patterns. This is a trait any ambitious person in the business world would kill for, because to be successful in business, it's essential to have a knack for identifying holes in the market, and then coming up with creative ideas that will fill those holes.

If you're an INFJ or INFP who avoided getting that business degree you might be asking what exactly a hole in the market is, but it's just another way of saying, "market opportunity." It's a problem people have that they need a solution for, and if you can come up with a good solution then you can provide that solution to all those people and be compensated for your great idea.

Usually, a good hole in the market points to a physical or logistical problem. For instance, the guy who invented Post-It Notes realized that it's super annoying to use lots of little pieces of tape to stick lots of little pieces of paper everywhere and he came up with a better solution. It's obvious to see how that worked out.

What isn't so obvious are the solutions to the new kinds of problems people are experiencing in this new kind of world. People need help like never before with *emotional* problems, and INFJs and INFPs are just the personality types equipped to find the solutions. There are so many people out there who need help dealing with grief, anger, past trauma, current relationship difficulties, and constant low self-esteem. Yes, some of these people will seek out traditional therapy and get help that way, but for a lot of others therapy isn't a good fit, either because they're resistant to that particular model of healing, or they can't afford it. INFJs and INFPs are the people who have the vision, creativity, and motivation to come up with new alternatives that can be accessed online, whether that be through offering a trauma workbook that people can work through at their own pace on Amazon, or posting videos on YouTube that lead people through guided meditations.

INFJs and INFPs have an amazing amount of potential to create the small businesses that can offer services to begin to heal people effectively. It will be the INFJs and the INFPs who figure out a way to build systems that emotionally support others as they go through illness, loss, old emotional baggage, and fears about the future. It will be the INFJs and INFPs who set the example of leadership in the heart-centered entrepreneur community. And with the level of technological innovation we're approaching, it's possible now to do all of this in a way that energetically *scales*—so that we as individuals can distribute our light to those who need it most, without getting drained ourselves.

Imagine an online business that specializes in emotional support. Imagine that it's run by a team of INFJs and INFPs who offer coaching, classes, therapy, forums, and other assorted resources for those who are in pain and need help. Imagine that each INFJ or INFP works on their own, and as part of the team, so they are able to do work they believe in, offer their gifts to the world, be provided with income that guarantees they thrive as a person, and also have ample time to spend on vacations, family, and their other creative pursuits.

Sound like a far-fetched dream? It could be a common reality. All it takes is for one of us to begin, and then another, and then for the two of us to band together. This is no dream, this is already happening. Slowly but surely, we are finding each other. We are reaching out and making connections. We are beginning to see what is really possible. Slowly but surely, we are starting to realize that in today's online world, anything could happen.

I believe it's no coincidence that almost every one of my INFJ or INFP clients tells me at some point that they're giving serious thought to striking out on their own and starting an online business. They've never felt at home in corporations, or any other workplace that focuses on rules and routines, and they've always felt this wild inner calling to do something big and creative, something that sounds risky but feels right to them on the heart level.

I understand what they're saying because I've always felt the same way, even 20 years ago when I was listening to all those grown-up English majors trying to convince me to take a normal job in the workaday world. But now, finally, I know it's possible to do something different. I know it's only a matter of time before we all find our niche, and it's not long before those dreams that seemed so far-fetched to us before become our normal, if not amazing, new reality.

CHAPTER 7
INFJs as Born Risk Takers: Mediocrity Is NOT an Option

In the summer of 2008 I quit my job with no contingency plan. I'd been working for a startup that offered media services to published authors and I had thought the job was exactly what I wanted. However, as I discussed in previous chapters, I quickly found out my boss was a narcissist and most definitely did not have the company's best interest at heart. I spent eight months there and I was miserable the entire time. Stressed, anxious, and always on the verge of a panic attack. Finally, I couldn't take it anymore. I woke up one morning in June and knew that was the day. I was quitting.

As usual, I had been living paycheck to paycheck. My boyfriend at the time, who is now my husband, was bartending, which was unreliable work with unreliable income. He knew how awful my job was and we had spent many an evening discussing options, of which there seemed to be few. But that morning when I decided to quit I knew I couldn't talk about it anymore. The toxic relationship I had with my boss was becoming dangerous to my health.

So, I quit. And it sucked, for a little while. For the next few months my boyfriend and I were broke. I knew I couldn't get another job right away either. The ordeal I had gone through with my toxic boss had traumatized me. I needed a little time to breathe, and to heal. I needed a couple of months off, at least. And, I needed to move.

I had spent the last four years in San Francisco, and I just didn't feel like I could stay in the city after what had happened. I wasn't sure if I was leaving forever, but I knew I needed to leave for now. My boyfriend agreed. We had originally met in Seattle, where he was from, and where we had both lived prior to moving to California. Seattle seemed to call to us now. It intuitively felt right. So, with no plan and no money, we vowed to make the move happen somehow.

Three months later, in September, we successfully landed back in the Pacific Northwest. I went out to lunch with a couple of old friends in Seattle's University District. One of the first things they asked me was what I wanted to do next.

"I don't know," I said truthfully. "I'll need to get a job for now, but I don't think I want a *job*-job in the future. I don't like working at a job. It's not fulfilling."

There was an uncomfortable silence at the table. I felt like I had said the wrong thing.

"Well..." one of my friends said slowly, "everyone has to work at a job."

My other friend chuckled nervously. "Um, yeah. I mean, you can't just *not* work."

I tried to explain that not working wasn't what I was talking about. I was talking about fulfillment. I was talking about finding—or creating—work that was meaningful to me, and that challenged and satisfied me on many different levels. It was to no avail. My friends remained puzzled throughout the entire meal.

It wasn't just this one conversation that let me know I was on a way different wavelength from a lot of other people. I got more negative feedback from other friends in reaction to the decisions I had made around my tumultuous year of working for my toxic boss, suddenly quitting, and then also just as suddenly embarking on a move back to Seattle. Some friends made it clear that they disapproved of me quitting a job with no backup plan in place. Others wondered if I should have stuck it out in San Francisco longer. Still others commented on me taking so much time off in between my last job and finding a new one. Everyone seemed to have an opinion, and all those opinions seemed to clash with what I knew was right for me.

I could understand my friends' confusion about my decisions. After all, on the surface, I appeared to be cautious. I was introverted, didn't like speaking without thinking, rarely joined in games or sports, and observed things for a long time before acting. But my careful exterior concealed a more authentic truth that was buried deep inside, and one that most others did not usually see.

I was actually a born risk-taker.

That's why my decision to suddenly quit my toxic job and move back to Seattle didn't surprise me, the way it seemed to surprise everyone else. And the strong intuitive insight I had that working at a traditional job in the future would never fulfill me didn't seem so odd either. I had always experienced these sudden epiphanies, these gut feelings that told me I *needed* to do a certain thing at a certain time, that I *had* to move in a certain direction, no matter what the risk, or how hard it was going to be.

In fact, the hardest part had nothing to do with taking a chance on all the risky things I had done in my past. It was dealing with the fallout from friends and family that I always experienced afterward.

For my whole life, in one way or another, it seemed like everyone around me was always trying to convince me to settle. All sorts of people had told me that I had to be content with a job I hated, or a relationship that was mediocre. Or they let me know that they didn't think my big idea (whatever that big idea was at the moment) would work and listed all the reasons why. I didn't get it. I never did this to people. Even in my darkest days when I was full of self-loathing, I still never shot down the hopes and dreams of others. Quite the opposite. When someone had what they thought was a big, brilliant idea, it turned me on and got me excited. I wanted to hear all about it. I wanted to dream about all the possibilities with them.

I've talked a bit about risk-taking and INFJs before, in my book *The INFJ Writer*. It's the idea that INFJs are capable of carrying out grand plans based on a lot of time carefully assembling the risk factors, and the pros and cons, of any possible course of action. But what I'm talking about now goes deeper than this, and it extends to INFP personalities too.

I believe that we INFJs and INFPs all have a great big fat streak of risk-taking in us. We have this streak not just because our different strains of intuition lead us to make reliably solid decisions, but also because we are people who are born thirsting to be fulfilled in this life. We don't want "just a job," we want work that feels like a calling, work that is highly compatible with our interests and abilities. We don't want "just a relationship," we want to fall in love with a soulmate. This insistence on living the life we want, the life we know we are capable of having, against all odds and anyone else's outside judgment, can easily cause a rift between us and most of the other people in mainstream society. The more we own what we really want, and the more we refuse to play along with accepting mediocrity as the best life has to offer, the more this rift will only widen.

I think this is why so many INFJs and INFPs become involved in the personal growth movement. In the past decade, there has been an explosion of online courses, seminars, blogs, webinars, and in-person retreats, classes, and bootcamps to help people shift their mindset, break through limiting beliefs, and finally go after their dreams, no matter how tough it might be to get there. INFJs and INFPs are deeply fulfilled by learning these types of things and teaching them to others, because at the core, we are brave souls, and deep down, we are born risk-takers. If true belief and the right heart energy are present, there is no one more willing than the INFJ or the INFP to take the leap off the cliff and trust that the Universe will catch them on the way down.

If you are an INFJ or an INFP and you've always felt a calling to help the world in some way, to be of service to humanity, but you're feeling stuck and you're not sure where to begin, look at your own life. Ask yourself the hard questions. Are you continuing to show up for a job you hate? Are you in a relationship that isn't good for either of you?

Have you spent who-knows-how-many years of your life wearing a mask and trying to fit in?

The first step toward helping the planet is helping yourself. You have to leave the job you hate, even if you don't have a contingency plan. Or, you have to create a new reality for yourself at that job so that your dynamic with it shifts and you're not being slowly poisoned by it every day. You need to break up with the person you don't love anymore, even if that means a messy divorce. You have to jump off the cliff, even if you're terrified that no one—much less the Universe—is going to catch you on the way down.

If you are an INFJ or an INFP, you have it in you to do this. You might not feel very strong right now, but you are among the strongest of human beings on earth. INFJs and INFPs are resilient like no one else. Trust me on this. I talk to hundreds of you, maybe more, every year and I've seen it. Every INFJ and INFP I have ever spoken with has gone through something that scarred them, and they got up again anyway and continued on with this crazy journey called life. Not only that, but they kept the commitment to fulfill their dreams—finding work they love, a partner who cherishes them for who they truly are, and a sense of self-worth that can't be shaken.

You can do it too. But you have to take the first step, you have to leave the old sucky thing behind before you can get to the new awesome thing. And you're going to have to deal with haters along the way, the people in your social circle who cannot understand what drives you or why you would risk job security or not having a date to your cousin's wedding, just to pursue the possibility of working in a career you love or holding out for the person you know you're meant for. The haters will always exist. It's not your responsibility to provide them with explanations for your decisions. What IS your responsibility is learning strategies to move past their negative energy so that you can invite new people into your personal community.

Look at your life right now. If you had total freedom, what would you change? Really think about it. Okay, now that you have that information, consider this: You *do* have total freedom. And on top of that, if you're an INFJ or an INFP, you also have tremendous insight, empathy, creativity, and intelligence. You don't have to stay stuck anywhere that you truly don't want to be.

So, do it. Take the risk. Jump off the cliff. You already know in your heart that it can be done. Now it's just a matter of letting yourself fall and trusting the Universe to catch you on the way down.

As terrifying as it is in the moment, I can promise you, taking the leap is worth it.

CHAPTER 8
The INFJ Revolution: Piece Together the Pattern, Use It to Help

It was a golden September afternoon and I was sitting in a ballroom packed with writers and artists at the El Dorado Hotel in Santa Fe, New Mexico. I had traveled there for a conference called Creative Reboot, specifically designed to help people reawaken their creativity and reconnect with themselves, tapping into the deepest parts of their creative hearts and souls to discover what brought them alive. I'd spent the weekend immersing myself in workshops on creativity, witnessing my fellow creatives walk across hot coals (literally, there was a fire walk), and exploring the colorful and eccentric little streets of downtown Santa Fe.

I'd been invited to the conference by a good friend of mine, Jacob Nordby. We had become friends after he read my first book, *The INFJ Writer*, and then emailed me about it. His message was so authentic and full of love that I instantly knew we were destined to be friends. Then, when I read his book, *Blessed Are the Weird*, I had even more confirmation. In *Blessed Are the Weird* Jacob talks about the poets, the misfits, the troubadours, the "weirdos" everywhere, who have always felt out of place, but who have also always had an important role to play in the world. Jacob put into words everything I had felt my entire life—the way I had deeply doubted myself for years, and also the small still voice within that I had sensed throughout everything, telling me that I did have a creative purpose, and it was a big one.

Jacob also happened to be an INFJ, and I had a hunch that most of the other people at Creative Reboot were probably INFJs, or INFPs, too. Seeing so many of us in one place was amazing, but not surprising. It seems that in recent years intuitive people have started to gather together at conferences and retreats, just like the one I was attending, like never before. For me, this was one more piece of the pattern of the worldwide INFJ movement, the ever-increasing trend of intuitive people discovering what they are, learning everything they can about it, and then using that knowledge to empower themselves and move forward in their lives.

Jacob's arrival into my life was another piece of my own personal pattern as it related to the INFJ movement. After publishing *The INFJ Writer*, I began to get messages from all kinds of INFJs over email and through social media. I also started taking on many more INFJ clients, who were intent on working with me because they were desperate for someone to understand their INFJ-ness, and how that played into their creative obstacles, and their creative triumphs.

I met one INFJ who had a neuroscience degree and had worked for years counseling people in the medical profession who were experiencing burnout. When she became burned out herself, she began looking deeper into the underlying pattern that might show her why so many people who were natural caregivers shut down after too many years of service. She used her intellect, intuition, and emotion—the whole INFJ package—to unearth the truth that the conventional medical community didn't want to see, that the spirit and emotions of a person have just as much impact on their health as the state of their physical body. She felt an exceptionally strong pull to uncover and heal this particular blind spot in the medical profession because of her own experiences as an INFJ, and also because she had worked with so many others who had been dismissed as "too sensitive," or who had been told to "get over it" when they couldn't go on with their work any longer.

I met another INFJ committed to exploring radical intimacy, and how our ideas around identity and relationships can grow and thrive if we work to become more accepting of all the different shapes and sizes both might take. Her vehicle of choice to fulfill this big purpose is male/male romance novels. She devotes herself to crafting each one of her books as a piece of art that not only entertains, but also enlightens her audience by tapping into their deepest emotions, while at the same time pushing them to think outside of their old familiar ideas about what love should look like.

One INFJ whom I met just last year is the creator of ASMR videos, which stands for Autonomous Sensory Meridian Response, popularly known as the "pins and needles" videos on YouTube. This INFJ discovered ASMR because she herself experienced it for many years, even though almost no one else knew what she was talking about when she tried to explain it. As a Highly Sensitive Person, she became aware that certain repetitive sounds stimulated a certain physiological response for her. I confided in her that I, too, have always had a special relationship with sound. I can pretty much immediately get a read on someone's personality just from hearing the sound of their voice. Instead of looking at me skeptically, which had often happened when I shared this with people in the past, this INFJ gave me a knowing smile. Then she gave me even more information about ASMR and we spent an enjoyable two hours discussing how it could help people.

Another INFJ—who is a longtime client and also a friend—wrote the memoir of her cousin, a woman who survived the murder of her family when she was only nine years old, and suffered the severe effects of trauma for years afterward. My INFJ client detailed her cousin's struggles with DID (Dissociative Identity Disorder) and how it was nearly impossible for her to find a therapist who could help her, or even acknowledge the existence of DID. I am constantly inspired by my client, as she works diligently to educate people on what her cousin went through and how she healed, a story that helps others who are going through similar struggles.

These are only a few of the stories I could tell about all the INFJs I have met in the three years since I published *The INFJ Writer*, there are dozens more. The number of stories isn't important though, it's the vein of gold that runs through each one and forms a pattern all its own. Of course, as an INFJ myself, I can see this pattern clearly. In fact, I couldn't miss it if I tried.

Every person has an emotional and spiritual center. Or maybe a layer. Maybe a core. Maybe it's not something that can be named or categorized, but it exists nonetheless. In Western society, this emotional, spiritual reality that exists in every person is largely dismissed, and those who believe in it are usually mocked by the more rationally-minded among us.

When my neuroscience INFJ was counseling people with burnout, she had a crazy difficult time getting anyone to listen to her ideas about how emotional and spiritual damage can result from taking on too much trauma from others, but that didn't break her commitment to helping people learn how to heal. My ASMR INFJ spends her professional life continuously explaining to others that ASMR is a real thing, and that sound carries the potential to affect us emotionally for good or ill. My male/male romance writer is a pioneer in her field as well, creating fictional relationships that open people to the possibility that there is more than one way for romantic and sexual relationships to take form. My memoir writer is also a crusader, showing others through her family member's story that trauma is something that can actually split the human spirit in two, and that the spirit is something you can heal only through the emotions.

There is a revolution going on right now, an INFJ revolution, and contrary to the label I've slapped on it, it involves more than just INFJ personalities. It's intuitive people overall, it's Highly Sensitive People, empaths and creatives and eccentrics. It's every person everywhere who has always known that emotions and energy are just as real and valid as logical thought and ideas. It's all those individuals who have been brave enough to create something that they know will help other people, at the same time running the risk of being dismissed, mocked, or outright ignored. In every era of history, there have been people ahead of their time. People with ideas that threatened the mainstream even if those very ideas could be the difference between a better world, or the next world war.

Many of these people are INFJs and INFPs. We have always been here, and we have always done what we do best: piece together the pattern, use it to help. But never before in history have we had access to each other like this. Never before have we known what we are and that there are so many others out there like us, that we are not alone. Never before have we been able to communicate with each other this quickly, or this powerfully.

People still think we're crazy, but that's okay. Because now we have each other. In centuries past, it would have been one or two of us, struggling alone, desperately trying to get people to listen to us, to see the pattern that we've put together, but now everything is different. When my ASMR INFJ gets flack for creating content that not that many other people understand, it's okay, because...the internet. There are millions more people out there who DO get it. The same goes for my memoir writer INFJ who is shining light on people who struggle with DID. Because of the online world we now live in, it really doesn't matter if mainstream psychology accepts this diagnosis or not. Everyone in the world with an internet connection has access to her book. They can read about her cousin's experience firsthand and decide if this is something that rings true for them.

We are entering a world in which we have a kind of freedom never before available to humankind. Information is instant. Knowledge is more than attainable, it's almost in overabundance. There are billions and billions of pieces of EVERYTHING floating out there, waiting for anyone to happen along and pick them up. And out of everyone on earth, it's the INFJs who are naturally wired to sift through so many different pieces and see the pattern.

INFJs, our time has come. Our time is now. There is no more waiting. If you're still holding back, then know that you are not being held back by anything outside of you. This is your time to not only shine, but to use your light to change the world. Our society is shifting in a way so that our intuitive, creative, compassionate, and magical gifts are finally welcomed. But it's up to each one of us to find our own voice, our own truth, and our own potential.

It's up to each one of us to stand up as an INFJ and embrace the big purpose that brings with it.

About the Author

Lauren Sapala is the author of *The INFJ Writer: Cracking the Creative Genius of the World's Rarest Type*, a writing guide for sensitive intuitive writers, and *Firefly Magic: Heart Powered Marketing for Highly Sensitive Writers*. She also writes transgressive fiction and currently lives in San Francisco. To find out more visit laurensapala.com.

Made in the USA
Monee, IL
07 February 2021

59906825R00104